40 "PROBLEMS" WITH CHRISTIANITY AND THEIR ANSWERS

BY
MG BENNETT

Copyright

©

2017 by MG Bennett. All Rights Reserved.

No part of this publication may be reproduced, distributed, or transmitted in any form or by any means, including photocopying, recording, or other electronic or mechanical methods, or by any information storage and retrieval system without the prior written permission of the publisher, except in the case of very brief quotations embodied in critical reviews and certain other noncommercial uses permitted by copyright law.

Some of the Most Common "Problems" With Christianity Fade Away In The Light Of Knowledge of Scripture

- MG Bennett

Contents

Introduction

1. Relative Time
2. Lack of Gradation
3. Barbaric Punishment
4. Hitler, Ted Bundy, and Bill Gates
5. Evil Nature of God
6. Transfer of Punishment
7. Belief Versus Actions
8. Infant death
9. Beginning of Life
10. Miracles
11. Failure to Return
12. Delayed Documentation
13. Fact Checking
14. Roman Bias
15. "Growing Fish"
16. Gospel Contradictions
17. Raising of Lazarus and Woman Caught in Adultery
18. Palm Sunday/Good Friday Conflict
19. Judas
20. Roman Census of Luke
21. Passover Prisoner Release
22. Other Gospel Books
23. Too many Messiahs
24. Two Gospels
25. Evolution Demarcation
26. Tiny Drama/Huge Stage
27. Chosen People
28. Ignored Scriptures
29. Jewish Fate
30. Prayer
31. Slavery
32. Homosexuality

33. Status of Women
34. Lack of Scientific Insight
35. Splintering
36. The Way Things Happen
37. Fictional Stories
38. The Ten Commandments
39. Borrowed Miraculous Elements
40. Too Many Problems

INTRODUCTION

There are various questions about the Christian faith, which have really good answers.

This is a comprehensive in range and yet easy to read book, written in the Spirit of God not just with mere logic because "Our struggle is not against flesh and blood" (Eph 6:12), which would boost your understanding and give you some good answers about the type of "problems" that hold many people not cross the Rubicon and come to God.

It will challenge you to know the Bible even better and prepare you not to be surprised, let alone stumped, at the hostile questions our secular culture is asking about our faith.

"40 "problems" with Christianity and their answers" responds and gives explanation to some of the most often asked questions and objections against the Christian faith.

Did Jesus fail to return?
Are the Gospels unreliable historically?
Were there too many Messiahs at and around the time of Jesus?
Is the Jewish fate too bleak for God to be real in their nation's history?
Does the Bible endorse slavery in any way?
Are women somehow second hand people from Biblical point of view?
Are there "ignored Scriptures", which should equally be part of the New Testament, but were rejected by the church on arbitrary grounds?
Is natural science really opposing the Bible?

These and 30 more purported "problems" with Christianity are discussed.

See what is wrong with these and many other questions/problems like this so you are able and "be prepared to give an answer to everyone who asks you to give the reason for the hope that you have. " (1 Peter 3:15)

The faith originated from God.
The faith is supernaturally dropped in your spirit!
The faith is incredibly reasonable if you approach it with the Spirit!
You can pass it to others!

(1) RELATIVE TIME

It makes no sense that the relatively short life we live on this planet, at most 100 years and perhaps as brief as a few minutes, would be used by a God to determine our ultimate destiny, one that will last trillions and trillions of years and beyond. This would be like compensating a baseball player for his entire career based on how he performs in his first major league at bat. If he hits a home run, he would receive a high salary, but if he strikes out, he will get only minimum wage throughout his career no matter how well he plays thereafter. The time difference between the trial period and the punishment/reward period is drastically out of sync.

Some Christians say that God will give people another chance after they die to accept his grace, but if that is true, then why be so concerned about the unsaved in this life? And if you get a second chance after you die, you will obviously know that Christianity is true, making the decision to believe not a matter of faith, but of fact. This makes no sense, and it would render the core theology of Christianity meaningless.

RESPONSE

Eternity is not an unlimited amount of time. Comparing time on earth with eternity is the wrong approach. Time is as old as about 13 billion years, if we go with modern science on this[1]. It cannot really be compared with eternity, which, in turn, is with no beginning and end and overlapping time.

---

[1] https://www.space.com/24054-how-old-is-the-universe.html accessed 22 Oct 2017

For example:

God is eternal and, crucially, the spirit he has put in every person is eternal too. The Bible says: "He has laid the eternity in their hearts (of humans)" (Ecclesiastes 3:11).

So thus posed, this objection is incorrect because it assumes that the eternal spirit needs time to take the right decision for God, and the longer this time is, the bigger chance that this person would finally decide to do the right thing and accept God.

Not at all! Some people need more time, but others do not and it is down to the individual, and it is known only to God how much time a person needs to come to repentance. Every human being is a spirit who dwells in a body, and somewhere in between the spirit and the body is the character (mind, will, and emotions) or the soul. The soul is formed and influenced, like the body is, by its environment.

When someone makes a decision for God, it could be the decision of the spirit (which has eternal repercussions) or a temporary position of the soul. What does that mean? Some people mentally agree with the Gospel and even go to church, but their hearts are not really obedient to God. They may fall out quite easily once they get tired of church life or believing, or they could stay in church all their lives but never really obey God.

Unless they root in their relationship with God deep into their spirit and thus become one with God - "whoever unifies himself with the Lord is one spirit with Him" (1 Corinthians 6:17). Same is for people who reject God and argue against Him with their mind and emotions but at some point, their spirit submits to His kind invitation. The eternal spirit needs to obey God first because that is what ultimately matters and then the soul and the body would follow suit. The decision of that eternal spirit is what determines the salvation of the person.

And surely, when the spirit is right before God, the sinful nature of that individual would always try to infect their saved spirit with disobedience and put it off the right and godly track. That is why we are warned to stay on "the narrow path" because when "sin develops it gives birth to death" (James 1:15), eternal death at that. Therefore, a person could live a short or a long life, but on both occasions, the spirit is given the opportunity to say 'yes' or 'no' to God and remain with God right to the end. If this decision turns out to be eternal, existential one of the spirit, not merely the soul and that person, stays with God here on earth, then he would inherit eternal life with Him.

So it's not the time that one lives here on earth that matters but as we said, the eternal decision of the everlasting spirit in the person made during their time on earth and manifested by the works of repentance and deeds done in faith and submission to God.

What happens to those who die as little babies or children? Traditionally, the church teaches that those are spirits which go back to God and enjoy His presence in an awaken or a semi-dormant state until the resurrection happens. They died before their body and mind were in a mature enough state to demonstrably accept or reject God (which, ultimately, would have been the decision of their spirit). Hence, God, being just and fair, would not let anyone die without a real chance to decide their own eternal fate.

We can trust God that everyone would be judged fairly and justly:

"Would not the Judge of the world do justice?" (Genesis 18:25).

(2) LACK OF GRADATION

Christianity proposes that only one of two fates awaits humans after they die — an extremely attractive invitation into Heaven or a miserable, dreadful sentence to Hell. Given the complexities and varieties of human experience, offering only two judgments is absurd.

People are born into many different circumstances, some with Bible-believing Christian parents and others with Muslim, Hindu, Jewish, or atheistic parents. Some were born during the Middle Ages when sectarian belief was ubiquitous versus the societies today which are much more secular. Some lived before the era of Christianity. Some were born with damaged mental capabilities. To shoehorn all of these people into a two-tiered judgment system is irrational.

Some Catholics believe in "purgatory" where souls can be purified before they are allowed to enter Heaven. This would seem to alleviate the problem somewhat if it weren't for the fact that it is completely made up without any basis in the Bible. However, it would also make the choices you make in this life much less meaningful if you could compensate for any shortcomings with a visit to purgatory. No matter how long the layover there, it would be infinitesimally short compared to the eternity that awaits in Heaven.

RESPONSE

Biblically, the author of the question is right, one doesn't need Purgatory to be made right before God. This happens through faith by "becoming one" with the death and the resurrection of

Christ. The "old man" dies alongside his sinfulness and the new person lives on in repentance by the grace of God as Christ lives on. He may be tempted to sin and indeed sin, but he will quickly come back to God, lay all before Him in full honesty and contrition, and receive forgiveness and grace. This process of constant repentance, as God instructs in the Lord's prayer, would make him stronger and also make his character purer, with no active sin in his life.

The punishments of God are two types in as much as the two main different groups of people (saved and unsaved) are concerned. With those who know him, he may discipline them and this would help them grow. Those who do not know him get the consequences of what they have done, but this is also usually designed to bring them closer to God. Although some people are beyond repair and they would resist coming to God for forgiveness and refuse forever to change their ways, but will stay on their course of being away from the good plan of God for them. Those people get punished eternally by God, letting them receive the natural consequences of their state of mind toward Him.

On either occasion, God does allow punishment reluctantly - "He does not inflict suffering to children of man from the heart" (Lamentations 3:33).

We distinguish two different kinds of punishment: temporal and eternal. Those punishments which happen on this Earth are not merely about 'getting the same' (retribution), but ideally, they are about correction and changing one's bad ways. God does not punish because He likes it and insists on the sinner getting what they deserve, but He does it with love, which is meant to discipline and bring a person closer to what is good for them and the other creation.

The eternal judgement is also broadly twofold: one for eternal separation from God and one which is the eternal enjoyment of closeness with God. Does it mean that all get the same punishment or same reward in all details as far as eternity is concerned? The Bible shows us that this is not the case. Jesus clearly said that some people would get bigger punishment: "Truly I tell you, it will be more bearable for Sodom and Gomorrah on the judgement day than for that city" (Matthew 10:15). We are not told what the degree of the nature of this punishment would be, but there is a differentiation and some people get worse than others because of the circumstances around their deeds and the gravity of their offenses on God's scale are worse. Similarly, Jesus said: "But lay up for yourselves treasures in heaven, where neither moth nor rust destroy..." He is implying here that we contribute to our eternal reward by being obedient here and active in His work. We are all saved by grace (Ephesians 2:8-9), but we all would receive our own particular reward in heaven from God in accordance with our works: "Behold, I am coming soon and in me is the reward which I will give to each in accordance with their deeds" (John 22:12). Also, we see that each of us would receive specific to our calling and work reward from God: "The one who plants and the one who waters have one goal and they will each get their reward according to their own labour" (1 Corinthians 3:8).

We can conclude that the Bible paints broadly two pictures of fate in heaven, but as the law of the land provides for punishment and reward for its citizens, similarly, God offers life with Him through the grace of Christ and its rewards based on our work for God or separation from Him and its consequences.

Within this broad framework, there is a lot of differentiation and we are all assessed individually on our merit or lack of it thereof.

(3) BARBARIC PUNISHMENT

Jesus mentions Hell or some derivative thereof many times in the gospels and hints that most people will end up suffering there (wide is the path of destruction). Here are some of the scriptures addressing Hell:

Matthew 5:28-29:
But I tell you that anyone who looks at a woman lustfully has already committed adultery with her in his heart. If your right eye causes you to stumble, gouge it out and throw it away. It is better for you to lose one part of your body than for your whole body to be thrown into hell.

Matthew 13:41-42:
The Son of Man will send out his angels, and they will weed out of his kingdom everything that causes sin and all who do evil. They will throw them into the blazing furnace, where there will be weeping and gnashing of teeth.

Mark 9:45-46:
And if your foot causes you to stumble, cut it off. It is better for you to enter life crippled than to have two feet and be thrown into hell.

A belief in Hell is unavoidable if one is to believe in Jesus. If Hell doesn't exist, then why would God have allowed it to be so prominently addressed in the Bible? This brings about an interesting comparison. Hitler sent Jews to the concentration camps and gas chambers for no reason other than their ethnic identity. This was a temporal punishment; it sometimes lasted only a few days. God, on the other hand, is prepared to send good, well-accomplished, and generous people to a place of everlasting punishment and torture for the crime of not believing in something for which no credible evidence exists. The God of the Bible is, in effect, worse than Hitler.

RESPONSE

Jesus talks in the Gospels about the peril of hellfire more than He does about paradise. He leaves no doubt that the lake of fire is a real place prepared for the devil and his angels. Sadly, many humans go there as well.

"Enter by the narrow gate. For the gate is wide and the way is easy that leads to destruction, and those who enter by it are many" (Matthew 7:3).

There is a dispute on whether or not most people ultimately get saved. At the time Jesus was saying those words, this was apparently the case, but Jesus came " to destroy the work of the devil"(1 John 3:8). Apostle John says this about Jesus in the context of people sinning and doing what is wrong before God, and how Jesus comes in person and turns them around by deleting their sins and regenerating them (renewing them through adding something new) for a new life for God. Also, Jesus Himself says that his followers should "therefore go and make disciples of all nations, baptizing them in the name of the Father, and of the Son, and of the Holy Spirit." (Matthew 28:19) This clearly shows a change of the whole game about the plight of the world.

I would not speculate if most people get saved but clearly God "desires all people to be saved and to come to the knowledge of the truth" (1 Timothy 2:4). It would not be totally surprising if most people make it to heaven, but this depends on if they will repent and come to God, and the church of God is called to get the good news to them and teach them how to live for God.

Hellfire is a very real and scary place, and Jesus leaves no doubt that this would be the plight of many people.

God would never send "good, well-accomplished, and generous people to a place of everlasting punishment." But if one rejects God and what He did through His Son and does that until the end of their days, then what they do is reject the Source of goodness and the most generous act ever done in the universe - God coming and being amongst us, experiencing evil to the point of untold suffering.

This state of mind is hardly "well-accomplished". Nobody who rejects God would be made to be with God by force. They may look like good people to us but God knows the hearts and the innermost motivations. Those who call upon the Name of the Lord would be saved. Those who are chosen to be with God would appreciate "the evidence," which, for the believers, is abounding. If the spirit of the person decided to obey God, then there would not be any serious issue with evidence. They would all have the experiential conviction to back up their faith claim.

Those who decided in their innermost spirit that they would reject the saving hand of God wouldn't be convinced by no evidence, even if an animal speaks to them (2 Peters 2:16, Numbers 22:28). The prophet, Balaam, here had heard and seen so much of the work of God in his life had to be stopped temporarily by his donkey appearing to talk to him. He was ultimately deemed to be killed by the Israelites because he loved this world more than the gift of God and was willing to compromise rather than obey God.

People are sometimes so wedded to their idea about reality that no evidence can change their mind. Richard Dawkins once famously said that he would not believe in God even if God appeared to him because he would think this is a hallucination[2].

Coming to God is a work of the spirit inside of man, but we should bear in mind that:

"The natural person does not accept the things of the Spirit of God, for they are folly to him, and he is not able to understand them because they are spiritually discerned." (1 Corinthians 2:14).

---

[2] https://www.spectator.co.uk/2008/03/if-god-proved-he-existed-i-still-wouldnt-believe-in-him/ accessed on 22 Oct 2017

Just rational or empirical evidence alone do not make people believe, but the response of the spirit in them to the call of God, which may happen at any time of their life, is the main reason why people believe. Some would prefer not to respond in kind, though, and their fate is eternal separation from God as per their choice.

(4) HITLER, TED BUNDY, AND BILL GATES

Related to the previous point, Christianity can be understood to endorse a spectacularly cruel and senseless outcome of how certain people are judged. All one has to assume is that Hitler, a Catholic by birth, understood the gravity of his sins and confessed them to Jesus before committing suicide. According to Christian doctrine, this simple act was sufficient for him to have *all* of his sins forgiven and to be welcomed into Heaven. On the other hand, the 6,000,000 Jews that he had murdered, and who by default failed to accept Christ, were sent to Hell. This is beyond unjust and irrational; it is unthinkable.

Similarly, Ted Bundy, a confirmed murderer of over 30 young women, confessed his sins before his execution and, according to Christian doctrine, was sent directly to Heaven.

On the other hand, Bill Gates, an atheist who has lived a virtuous life and has donated more than $27,000,000,000 to global health, development, and education will be sent to Hell. This irrational and senseless result is entirely consistent with the dogma of conventional Christianity.

RESPONSE

We established in the previous entry that no one goes to heaven by being forced and surely no one would go to hell (which is being eternally separated from God) because God wants this.

Genuine repentance of a sinner without an opportunity for good deeds, which usually authenticate the new commitment is only accessible to God to appraise. The bandit on the cross did not have time to show that he truly turned to God, but Jesus promised him that he would be in paradise nonetheless (Luke 23:39-43).

We cannot know if Hitler might have repented in the very end and got saved. But that development is very unlikely because we have reasonable reasons to believe that he committed suicide[3]. This shows that his hypothetical repentance, if there was such thing at all, was not sincere. If he repented and got killed by a bomb, then only God knows how sincere he was, and based on how genuine his repentance was (for the sake of the argument), God would have granted him forgiveness. That shows how gracious and generously forgiving God is and how the power of the blood of Jesus is being sufficient to remove all sins.

This, of course, also show how someone who could eventually be saved could do so much harm due to the lies of the sin which he followed. It is possible that a person wastes his life and cause harm to himself and many others, and although he loses a lot of what he can have on earth and the rewards in heaven, but still, he gets eternal life in any moment. That's why we should warn all people of the perils of sin, which ruins their life and consumes their time, inflicting creative and spiritual infertility.

I hasten to add that it is only marginally possible in my view that people like Hitler might have awakened in the last moment and turned away from their despicable deeds for good so they could receive forgiveness. A sinful life is a symptom of spiritual death and the longer you go with it the more sin develops. "When sin develops fully, it brings death" (James 1;15). If one has not come to God all their life and gave themselves to utter evil instead, it does not seem very likely they would call to Him in the very end.

Once more, if and when this happens, it shows the glorious opportunity to give yourself to God for the eternity not being missed, and how good God is to those who truly come to Him.

---

[3] http://www.history.com/this-day-in-history/adolf-hitler-commits-suicide-in-his-underground-bunker accessed on 22 Oct 2017

Now, if Hitler is unlikely to have repented, there are surely people who do repent after serious transgressions. We mentioned the bandit on the cross next to Jesus who was sorry and asked for forgiveness and received it.

How about Bill Gates and people who do a lot of good things but never accept Jesus as a personal savior? Bill Gates lives a much more decent life than Ted Bundy ever did before he came to God, but he would be judged first and foremost, as every person would be, based on how he responded to God's message of love and call to turn to Him. If he had ever been presented with the Gospel, and the Holy Spirit prompted him to repent, and then he accepted that his achievements come to nothing in the grand scheme of eternity and the holiness of God, and he accepted that what matters is if he reconciled himself with His Creator by God's Son, then he would've been saved, like any other person - by grace, through faith. His good works would determine the rewards he would get and the position he would have in the eternal kingdom of God, but he would not enter the kingdom because he earned it with good deeds. This would mean that people can be perfect before God without His grace and that Jesus died in vain. Human beings are incapable of reaching and maintaining the high standard of God by themselves. This is fundamental to Christianity.

The Bible clearly says that if they think otherwise, they are either ignorant, not realizing how high this standard is, or arrogant, by thinking that they have attained it by their own strength or both.

If Bill Gates rejects the Gospel, then this means He rejects the only way he can get to heaven. His good works are commendable but insufficient because the only way to get there is faith first and then good works. Faith means relationship and that is what God is after.

(5) EVIL NATURE OF GOD

Christians have tried to sidestep the evil deeds that God allegedly commits in the Old Testament by claiming that the New Testament overrides and replaces the Old Testament, based on the idea that Jesus supplied mankind with a new covenant. This is somewhat understandable, but what cannot be denied is that Jesus himself was a student of the Old Testament, firmly believed in it, and warned that it was not to be ignored or discarded.

Given the Christian belief that Jesus was God, then in order for Christianity to be true, Jesus/God must have performed the evil deeds as documented in the Old Testament. Otherwise Jesus would have corrected the scriptures and explained that God the Father (or He Himself?) did not commit those atrocities. To repeat, according to Christians, Jesus was God, and he was physically on Earth teaching from the Old Testament. If the scriptures were wrong in their portrayal of God, Jesus would have emphatically announced this fact to his followers and whoever else would listen.

The following is taken from Steve Wells' *Drunk with Blood: God's Killings in the Bible*, listing 158 killing events for which God was either directly or indirectly responsible. A partial list is shown below for effect, but one in particular deserves a focused look, 1 Samuel 15:3:

Now go, attack the Amalekites and totally destroy all that belongs to them. Do not spare them; put to death men and women, children and infants, cattle and sheep, camels and donkeys.

Jesus did nothing to defend or denounce this scripture, and apparently it was consistent with his concept of God the Father.

The case can be made that God killed or authorized the killings of up to 25,000,000 people. This is the God that Jesus looked up to and of whom he was allegedly an integral part. That is to say: Jesus himself was an accessory to these massacres. Therefore, Christianity cannot extract itself from these atrocities; it must own them and admit that their God is in fact a serial, genocidal, infanticidal, filicidal, and pestilential murderer.

RESPONSE

Let's be clear - God the Father and Jesus are One God. Therefore, whatever is attributed by the Bible to the Father is done by the Son and vice versa. Therefore, everything that God did in the Old Testament is also a deed of the God in the New Testament.

God can do everything He likes and He is always right; everything He does is the best possible course of action. He showed His immense love, and that He is keen to save the whole world (John 3:16) by sending His Son to it, but not all people would choose to receive His salvation (John 3:33).

Sometimes, evil develops so much that it threatens God's good plan for other human beings. God would stop it by letting the evil people, whom He spared a great deal of bad things, suffer the consequences of their evil works.

"So I gave them over to their stubborn hearts to follow their own devices" (Psalm 81:12).

God is good and He doesn't want human beings to go through suffering, though.

"For he does not enjoy hurting people or causing them sorrow" (Lamentation 3:33).

He is so good that He let His Son (who is an integral part of God) to be subjected to unfair punishment and torment, thus taking all the evil that the world has ever conceived and done upon Himself. He offers His love and salvation from the evil nature of humanity and hell freely to all people. Those who choose to reject it would have to take the result of what their "own devices" led them choose, do, and endorse.

If the loving God got to the point where he had to kill so many people for their sins (the Flood for example), then this is the best thing He can do for humanity at this point. The human race had to be euthanised in order to save a few who would propagate it later on. God has given people free will, which makes it impossible to make them do what is right unless they respond from their own volition to God's invitation.

Only on two occasions has God used His people to inflict direct judgement on a group of people (Canaanites and Amalekites) and the reason is that they were in a very close proximity to the inadvertently erring and sinning nations and had to take it on themselves to punish evil or it could engulf them. The options for the evil doers were opened, though - they could repent from the evil in their hands and become followers of God or they could just flee from the land.

But these are two exceptions. We have no indication in the Bible, henceforth, that this is a standard way of dealing with sinful groups of people, and on the contrary, God said, "Love your enemy" (Matthew 5:44).

God gave all people in history a telling example with those nations how decisive His people should be against evil and sin and how bad and unacceptable evil is, but He reserves the ultimate judgement of the world for Himself.

The Christians are called alongside everyone else who sympathises with Jesus' words to indeed love their neighbours and pray for their good and salvation.

(6) TRANSFER OF PUNISHMENT

Christians believe that Jesus died for their sins and received the punishment that they would otherwise deserve. At its root, this is unethical. It would be as if in a court of law, a murderer sentenced to death finds another person willing to die in his place, and the murderer is then set free. Why would we accept God's plan of salvation while categorically not using a similar rationale in our own judicial system? Well, because it is ill-advised, and it leads to the next problem.

RESPONSE

We have to clear up a couple of misunderstandings here. First, Jesus is not just "another person" who is sacrificed for the sins of others. That would be wrong before God as every soul would bear "its own sin" (Ezekiel 18:20). Jesus is God.
Also, secondly, all sins committed are ultimately done against God: "To you, you only, have I sinned and done what is evil in your sight; so you are right in your verdict and justified when you judge" (Psalm 51:4).

God has created mankind with lots of love and made them righteous (Eccl 7:29), and every deviation from the initial state of innocence runs against God's plan and will. This would make Him suffer because it is not His will that anyone would perish.

Men had fallen but the image of God is in every human being and some respond to His call to come to Him and be restored.

The analogy with the human judicial system is inappropriate because it's not merely a human being who was crucified for the sins of the world but God's eternal Word, the God-man, the Son of God, who is God and one with the Father. The evil acts of the world could be taken up and paid for by the Creator because, ultimately, they were all acts against Him.

In the human court system, if one man takes the penalty for the sins of another, this would mean anarchy as it wouldn't be edifying to the rest of the society. It would also mean that the culprit may well remain the same bad person, but even bolder in his evil deeds knowing that it could be all remedied as long as someone agrees to take it for him.

When God sacrifices Himself, then God's love is acting as per His loving character by taking a contradiction against His divine nature in order to put a break to the ongoing offences against Him. It ensures that the punishment for sin is meted out justly, but in reflection of His character, He is reluctant to afflict evil to the perpetrator and gives a chance to everyone to avoid it.

The death of Christ as substitute shows that God has done all that He could do in love and justice to make our sins go away.

Many people are and would be touched by the love of God and His willingness to have mankind come back to Himself and this serves to teach humanity how to be good more than all the punishments ever carried out by the judicial system. Often, people re-offend and go back to their sinful ways after they serve their time, but one who truly recognise and receive this love would be a thoroughly changed person.

This act of God sends a message that the One whom all bad deeds are committed against is willing to generously pardon, and He is offering forgiveness and help to the evil one in order to change them. God is the only one who can take the sin of another because He concentrates as an ultimate receiver of all evil works ever done by anybody. So, is the punishment greater if this "great salvation" is neglected and despised?

"How much more severely do you think someone deserves to be punished who has trampled the Son of God underfoot, who has treated as an unholy thing the blood of the covenant that sanctified them, and who has insulted the Spirit of grace?" (Hebrews 10:29).

(7) BELIEF VERSUS ACTIONS

Christianity credits what you believe far above what you do. This idea has caused much misery and suffering over the course of the past two millennia. The notion that what you believe can erase your bad deeds is a very attractive idea to someone who wants to take liberties with the lives and property of other people. And this is exactly what happened during the scourges of the Inquisition and other atrocities committed by Christians. How different would the world be if Christianity instead declared that your ultimate reward is based on your actions, what you do, how you conduct your life, how much you help others, etc. instead of offering this exceptionally generous "Get Out of Jail Free" card? What if it said all of the good you do is balanced against the bad, and you would be judged based on that comparison?

RESPONSE

The Bible reveals a unique picture of the process of salvation. It depicts God, who is holy and perfect, and humans, who, due to being in a fallen spiritual state, cannot satisfy His high standard with their works. The gulf between God's high standards of morality and spiritual existence is bridged only through His grace and by faith in the blood. "Abraham believed in the LORD, and He counted it to him as righteousness" (Gen 15:6). It is like a bank account which is heavily into overdraft, and God in His love credits it with a vast amount and then hands you again the responsibility of how to spend the money.

Here comes the role of the works. We get justified by faith alone but we get saved through faith, which produces works once God's righteousness is imputed to us by our faith.

"What good is it, my brothers, if someone says he has faith but does not have works? Can that faith save him?"
"So also faith by itself, if it does not have works, is dead."
- James 2: 14 and 17

James is clear that the grace could be misused and the faith rendered it useless if it is not accompanied by good works done through the power of God in us. The works validate the faith's sincerity and truthfulness. We don't do good works in order to pile up enough of them to get saved, but we do good works because we are already saved, and if we don't practice the faith we profess, this gift of salvation could be invalidated.

Jesus on many occasions says how important it is to produce good works of faith.
"In the same way, let your light shine before others, so that they may see your good works and give glory to your Father who is in heaven."
- Matthew 5:16

This light is the light kindled through faith but it cannot be hidden from the world to see it.

"Not everyone who says to me, 'Lord, Lord,' will enter the kingdom of heaven, but the one who does the will of my Father who is in heaven."
- Mathew 7:21

This addresses the people who don't want to repent and to walk rightly before God but call upon His Name. His response is uncompromising - "Repent" - and a loving one - "I am with you every step of the way," and "You don't have to do it alone I will help you." Based on our repentance and faith, we receive salvation. And based on our works, we affirm our salvation and receive eternal rewards.

"Behold, I am coming soon, bringing my recompense with me, to repay each one for what he has done."

- Revelation 22:2

God wants to forget all the bad stuffs we have done and remember and reward all the good things we have done. If anyone wants to keep doing what is evil before God after they have known the truth, then this would deplete their credit of grace and they would have to take the consequence of all their deeds. God is gracious and good but His kindness shouldn't be abused. To the weak, He gives strength, to the headstrong, He says, be "humble and repent," and to the deceived, He says, "I will teach you the path you have to walk into." (Psalm 32:8) His kindness leads us to repentance (Romans 2:4). When not appropriated in obedience, it remains handed down in vain.

(8) INFANT DEATH

Most Christians believe that people who die at a young age are given a free pass to Heaven. This is a comforting thought, but it makes for some peculiar considerations. It would seem to suggest that dying at a young age, before encountering the age of accountability, would be the best and safest way to leave Earth. This would guarantee a place in Heaven without having to take a risk of living a potentially failed life in the sight of God. Some demented parents have exploited this idea as an excuse to murder their children.

RESPONSE

The Bible says that God has determined the number of days for each person.
"Your eyes saw my unformed substance; in your book were written, every one of them, the days that were formed for me, when as yet there was none of them."
- Psalm 139:16

Only God should decide how many days one should live. This goes for unborn babies as well because His eyes "saw my unformed substance". Before the zygote was formed, God knew the number of days this human being would have to live. Nobody should take it upon themselves to sever the life of another as this runs directly against God's prerogatives. God is a life-giver and His will is that everyone lives their full number of days. He counted the days of each one of us, but the Bible also startlingly reveals to us that God has determined a number of good works that each of us should do on this earth.

"For we are his workmanship, created in Christ Jesus for good works, which God prepared beforehand, that we should walk in them."
- Ephesians 2:10

This life appears to be an opportunity for every person to make a choice to obey God, and through faith to fulfil all the good things that God planned for them. If one has done all God wanted him/her to do, this means they have lived a fulsome and satisfying life and have realised their full God-given potential.

The Bible does not focus on the negative but on the positive. This life is incredibly important and should be lived to the full of God's will. It is not a risk to fail and lose the eternal life with God but an opportunity to glorify God. It's true that only a demented or evil person would want to stop such a great unfolding of destiny, which human life represents.
If an infant dies on their own, this should be of natural causes, and we know that God has taken someone who would be with Him, but a baby should never pass away due to human intervention because they have to be given a chance to live for God.

(9) BEGINNING OF LIFE

Many Christians believe that life begins at conception

and an entire anti-abortion industry has been built around this concept. But it presents a problem. Does a fertilized egg that fails to implant in the uterus go to Heaven? This seems a bit absurd, but it is important to consider in the context of Christian dogma. If one assumes this is not the case, then it becomes very difficult to identify when a developing fetus becomes eternal in the eyes of God. Is it at the moment of birth, such that a baby that dies just before delivery is denied Heaven? There is no non-arbitrary way to solve this problem.

RESPONSE

This problem is more an issue of minutia detail than a real problem. Difficult cases make for bad basis for distilling a guiding principle or a law.
God said that:
"Therefore a man shall leave his father and his mother and hold fast to his wife, and they shall become one flesh."
- Gen 2:24

They become "one flesh" intimately, but they become one flesh through the conception of each of their children. That's why the church believes that life begins from the moment the masculine and the feminine meet and join at this very deep and organic level. When the biological parts of man and a woman meet and join in this way, then a new spirit is given by God and a new human is created with its potential but also with the perils to their existence which surround every person (in this case, failing to bed into the mother's womb). Whatever happens later wouldn't stop the generated spirit, which makes life possible, from coming back to God if the vehicle of the biological body fails to carry it to a fully-fledged existence.

Life, which begins from conception, is the only non-arbitrary starting point for it because there and then, the two parts become one and form something which did not exist before, and which is genetically different from both halves on their own, and, thus, makes a unique human.

All other points of time and development suggested when humanity begins (if the mother wants it, first breath, etc.) are practically indefensible and arbitrary.

(10) MIRACLES

Many Christians accept at face value that Jesus' miracles as described in the Bible were true historical events. However, these alleged miracles occurred in Roman-occupied lands, and the Romans had spies that attended large gatherings of Jews to detect any whispers of insurrection. News of these miraculous events, especially feeding thousands with only five loaves of bread and two fish (Matthew 14:13-21), would have spread rapidly all around the empire and eventually to the Roman emperor. It is hard to imagine that the Romans would not have investigated these extraordinary phenomena, documented it in their written accounts, and perhaps have tried to determine if Jesus or his methods could be used to solve some of the problems of the empire. The lack of Roman documentation of the miracles makes their historicity highly suspect.

RESPONSE

Jesus's miracles were such that great crowds were following him. He was indeed trying to ensure that they don't spread His glory far and wide and most of the time it appears He was asking those who received healing or deliverance from Him not to talk about it.

In Mark 1:41, 42, He told the healed leprous man, "Don't tell anyone."

In Matthew 8:27- 31, He told the formerly blind man not to tell anyone again.
In Matthew 16:18-20 and Mark 8:27-30, He told them not to tell anyone that he is the Messiah.

He knew that the more His fame is spread, the more pressure and opposition He would face. In Mark 1:45, we read that He "could not openly enter a town but withdrew to desolate places." Ultimately, by becoming incredibly famous in Judea and maintaining His uncompromising message, He brought to Himself the fate which the Scripture predicted about Him - he was arrested and killed. He had avoided this for about 3 years, during which he could train His disciples and pass on His teaching.
Part of His strategy to escape the problems coming his way sooner than necessary was to ask for the discreet handling of what they have seen and experienced. Had He not said this at all, we could imagine that the frenzy around His ministry and miracle working would have been even more significant. Some people seek fame by all possible means and this is what his brothers thought about Him. He tried to avoid getting too much of it because His works spoke volumes anyway to all who were blessed enough to see and hear them.
From the Romans' perspective, though, in as much as they were aware, He was undoubtedly one of the many charismatic teachers around the Empire, who, although now generally forgotten, we know about from history annals. One example is Appolonius of Tyana who lived in the first century AD and was called "son of the gods," and reportedly did numerous miracles, like the healing of the sick, casting out demons, raising dead people, etc. Whatever he was doing, though, it did not start a movement that changed the world and it seems he could not pass it onto his students, and after being killed by the Romans,

he was forgotten over time.[4] Throughout the empire, there were many people who claimed, or others claimed about them, to be miracle workers, and most likely, He was thought to be one of those, so His works initially didn't raise any eyebrow.

Also, shortly after he started off His work, only 3 years into his full ministry, He was captured and given up to punishment by crucifixion. There was no time for a reliable and verified news of His abilities to filter through amongst all others and reach the Emperor in Rome, who in turn had many other challenges to think about and attend to and little time to ponder about a charismatic religious teacher, a monotheist at that (!) in a small province along the Eastern Mediterranean shores.

Jesus' works and words stood the test of time, but from the point of view of the Empire, He was one of many.

---

[4] Erhman, Bart. D. A Brief Introduction to the NT, OUP, 2009, p15

(11) FAILURE TO RETURN

Biblical historians are quite clear on this matter. Early Christians — notably Jesus, Paul, the disciples, and other followers — were all convinced that the End Times were near and that Jesus himself would return to Earth within the generation of some of the people who were currently alive. The Bible claims that Jesus made the following comment in Matthew 16:28:
"Truly I tell you, some who are standing here will not taste death before they see the Son of Man coming in his kingdom."
Jesus also advised against going to court against someone who steals something and also told people not to store up stocks or reserves for the future. Clearly, he also thought the end was very near.
For the same reason, Paul advised followers not to marry. In the passage below, he obviously believes that some of the people he is talking to will still be alive for the Second Coming:
"For the Lord Himself will descend from heaven with a shout, with the voice of the archangel, and with the trumpet of God; and the dead in Christ shall rise first. Then we who are alive and remain shall be caught up together with them in the clouds to meet the Lord in the air, and thus we shall always be with the Lord. Therefore comfort one another with these words." (1 Thessalonians 4: 16-18)
The obvious fact is that the Second Coming was not in

fact forthcoming or even close to being near. The 2,000-year delay is a strong piece of evidence that Christianity is a failed religion.

The following quotation from Stephen L. Harris, Professor Emeritus of Humanities and Religious Studies at California State University — Sacramento, completes this point with a devastating argument. Remember that Jesus was a Jew who had no intention to deviate from the Hebrew scriptures:

"Jesus did not accomplish what Israel's prophets said the Messiah was commissioned to do: He did not deliver the covenant people from their Gentile enemies, reassemble those scattered in the Diaspora, restore the Davidic kingdom, or establish universal peace… Instead of freeing Jews from oppressors and thereby fulfilling God's ancient promises — for land, nationhood, kingship, and blessing — Jesus died a "shameful" death, defeated by the very political powers the Messiah was prophesied to overcome. Indeed, the Hebrew prophets did not foresee that Israel's savior would be executed as a common criminal by Gentiles, making Jesus' crucifixion a "stumbling block" to scripturally literate Jews…"

Jesus' immediate followers, mostly his 12 disciples, probably did not immediately identify this failure, because after Jesus' body was likely stolen and concealed, a rumor spread that Jesus had been resurrected from the dead. A sense of optimism overcame their grief about his execution and renewed some hope that he was a true messiah. If they had known then that there was to be no return in the near or long-term future, they likely would have abandoned any further activity. Despite this resurgence in their faith, they never agreed with Paul's concept of Jesus as being divine. Anything written in the Bible to suggest that they did is probably a result of later editing by some of Paul's followers. Such a belief would have been an exceptional departure from the Jewish faith.

RESPONSE

It is true that the early disciples expected Jesus' return imminently. That is what He told them to do:
"Therefore keep watch, for you do not know on what day your Lord comes."
- Matthew 24:42.

How could they keep watch if they didn't expect Him at any moment? This sense of imminence helped them live their lives in full obedience and devotion. Obviously, they also knew that certain events should happen first before Jesus comes back.
Apostle Paul said in 2 Thessalonians 2:3: "Let no one deceive you in any way. For that day will not come, unless the rebellion comes first, and the man of lawlessness is revealed, the son of destruction."
He clearly points out that Jesus' second coming and the resurrection of the dead in Christ would not happen before there is a resurgence of "lawlessness," i.e., rife deviation from the teachings of the Bible which culminates with the appearance of the "man of lawlessness" - Antichrist. However, they all had to be "watchful" and, hence, Paul talked about "we" when describing these future events. He didn't say that no one should marry because there is no point at all "as the time is short" (it is short indeed - there is one lifespan for each person before they meet the Eternal Judge), but he said that this vigilance should be our first priority ahead of all the other concerns we may have in life. Jesus also didn't instruct that people sell all their possessions for good, but that they are willing to share their material blessings with those in need.
Furthermore, He said that He doesn't know when the day would be. "But concerning that day and hour no one knows, not even

the angels of heaven, nor the Son, but the Father only" (Matthew 24:36). It was not God's will that they know when that day would be. Being in human form, Jesus didn't know absolutely everything supernaturally, although he could if he wanted. We read that He "learnt" by natural means and sometimes choose not to know things or possess powers in principle belonging to Him.

He told them about the incoming destruction of the temple of Jerusalem and predicted that it would happen before His coming again. "As for these things that you see, the days will come when there will not be left here one stone upon another that will not be thrown down." (Luke 21:6)

Similarly, Apostle Peter was told that he would get "old" and die for the truth of the Gospel meaning he would not see the second coming:

"I tell you the truth, when you were younger you dressed yourself and went where you wanted; but when you are old you will stretch out your hands, and someone else will dress you and lead you where you do not want to go" (John 21:18).

This all meant that there was going to be some (unknown) period of time before the Second Coming takes place which they knew about. Yet, they were told they should expect it any moment and be on their "watch". Did any of them see the Son of Man coming in His Kingdom then?

In Matthew 16:28 Jesus said:

"Truly I tell you, some who are standing here will not taste death before they see the Son of Man coming in his kingdom."

Yes, because the story continues:

1 And after six days Jesus took with him Peter and James, and John his brother, and led them up a high mountain by themselves.

2 And he was transfigured before them, and his face shone like the sun, and his clothes became white as light.

3 And behold, there appeared to them Moses and Elijah, talking with him.

- Matthew 17:1-3

They saw Jesus become transfigured before their eyes and speaking with the prophets of old - Moses and Elijah - the limitations of time and matter were made superfluous because the Kingdom of God which is originating in the spiritual realm descended upon them right then:
"...behold, a bright cloud overshadowed them, and a voice from the cloud said, "This is my beloved Son, with whom I am well pleased; listen to him." - Matthew 17:5

Thus, indeed, some of them "standing" there and listening experienced and saw "the Son of Man in His kingdom" as Jesus informed them 6 days earlier that it would happen.
In light of this, how do we interpret the verse: "Truly I tell you, this generation will certainly not pass away until all these things have happened" (Matthew 24:34)? Is it the generation which lived then? It cannot be so because most, if not all, of them had passed away when John was writing the Revelation in c.95 AD and describing future events.
It could not be the case because Jesus said, "This Gospel of the Kingdom would be preached around all the world for a witness to all nations and then the end will come" (Matthew 24:14). Clearly, they needed more time before all people are reached with the Good News. So "this generation" means the type of people and the generation of rejectors of God who would not pass until the end comes.

In the end, a few words about the Messiah and what kind of anointed leader the Jews expected. In a nutshell, they hoped for a political leader, genius, who would save Israel from all their troubles and inaugurate a world peace. Many of them believed He would rule, but it's not clear if all thought that his dynasty or his own reign would endure forever. For the most part, He would be a human king who does what God wants.[5]

In the book of Samuel, though, God clearly says that He wants to govern His people directly and the institution of the monarchy is not something which He was happy to endorse.
"And the Lord told him: "Listen to all that the people are saying to you; it is not you they have rejected, but they have rejected me as their king. 8 As they have done from the day I brought them up out of Egypt until this day, forsaking me and serving other gods, so they are doing to you."
- 1 Samuel 8:7,8

There is something here about a man ruling over God's people even in the name of God which God says He dislikes. "They have rejected me as their King," He says.

And then later on we read:

17 Is it not wheat harvest today? I will call upon the LORD, that he may send thunder and rain. And you shall know and see that your wickedness is great, which you have done in the sight of the LORD, in asking for yourselves a king. 18 So Samuel called upon the LORD, and the LORD sent thunder and rain that day, and all the people greatly feared the LORD and Samuel.
- 1 Samuel 12:17-18

Clearly, God wants to be the King over those who accept Him in a direct and intimate manner.
That will happen when Christ comes back to put down the forces of evil and herald His Kingdom on earth.

---

[5] http://www.jewishvirtuallibrary.org/the-messiah accessed on 22 Oct 2017

On top of it, something which the Jewish tradition did not always agree on, Messiah had to suffer for the sins of the world, and Isaiah 53 and other texts in the Old Testament so vividly portray this important work He would do.

"But He was pierced for our transgressions; he was crushed for our iniquities; upon him was the chastisement that brought us peace, and with his wounds we are healed."
- Isaiah 53:5

Therefore, the Messiah, before He enters His glorious reign, had to suffer for the sins of all and then he would be able to give repentance to Israel as per God's plan.

"And I will pour out on the house of David and the inhabitants of Jerusalem a spirit of grace and pleas for mercy, so that, when they look on me, on him whom they have pierced, they shall mourn for him, as one mourns for an only child, and weep bitterly over him, as one weeps over a firstborn."
- Zechariah 12:10

Israel would look for salvation to Him whom they have "pierced" and mourn for Him and repent. Who is the best candidate to fulfil all this? Only God in flesh, Jesus of Nazareth, the eternal Son of God who became Son of Man and lives forever being an organic part of God, the Word of God, and God Himself could fulfil everything which the prophets spoke about the Messiah.

13 "In my vision at night I looked, and there before me was one like a son of man,[a] coming with the clouds of heaven. He approached the Ancient of Days and was led into his presence. **14** He was given authority, glory and sovereign power; all nations and peoples of every language worshiped him. His dominion is an everlasting dominion that will not pass away, and his kingdom is one that will never be destroyed."
- Daniel 7:13,14

(12) DELAYED DOCUMENTATION

The accounts of Jesus' life in the gospels were written well after the events allegedly occurred. The crucifixion of Jesus is believed to have occurred around 30 AD. The best estimates date the gospels as follows:
Mark: AD 68-73
Matthew: AD 70-100
Luke: AD 80-100
John: AD 90-110
The time lag between the events and the documentation was long enough for exaggeration and myths to contaminate the historical account. It would be similar if a person today wrote a biography of Dr. Martin Luther King, Jr. just by talking to people who heard something about him from their now-deceased ancestors.

RESPONSE

The general scholarly consensus, which includes sceptical and traditional scholars, is that Jesus died around the year 30 AD. The earliest written New Testament books were some of the epistles of Apostle Paul (converted around 34 AD) in the late 40ies and 50ies. This means that less than 5 years after the death and resurrection of Jesus of Nazareth and within 20 years of it, Paul is respectively preaching Christ, and a little later, writing his letters. Indeed, this is very soon and after the events occurred, he assured his listeners that most people who saw Jesus resurrected are still alive and all the apostles who were with Jesus agreed with his teachings.

"Then He appeared to more than five hundred brothers at one time, most of whom are still alive, though some have fallen asleep." (1 Corinthians 15:9).
"As for those who were held in high esteem--whatever they were, makes no difference to me; God does not show favoritism--they added nothing to my message." (Galatians 2:6-10).

James, the brother of Jesus, and especially apostle Peter preached Christ, even earlier in the very early 30ies and then wrote about Jesus well before the 60ies when they were put to death.

The Gospel of Mark was written (if we follow secular scholarship) around the year 70 AD, which is the year when Jerusalem was sacked by the Romans. It is likely that Mark wrote before year 70, and traditional scholarship even suggest 50ies and early 60ies, but we would stick with the generally secular, accepted time frame, for the sake of the argument. This means that the first written gospel was published just 35-40 years after Jesus died on the cross, which is very close to the events, but it is assumed by most scholars that the oral tradition went back right to that period, which it is describing.[6]

Luke, in turn, was Paul's very close companion, who is the earliest NT writer. Matthew and Luke were written, as per the academic consensus, sometime in the 80ies (this dating is again disputed by the traditional and other scholars, but we would take this sceptical view and address the traditional one in the next chapter).

As it would seem, they used Mark's work extensively because there are a lot of overlapping events described in Mark that they both mention or that they may have worked relatively independently but were all sufficiently close to the authentic stories.

---

[6]

https://www.bc.edu/schools/stm/crossroads/resources/birthofjesus/intro/the_dating_of_thegospels.html accessed on 22 Oct 2017

We cannot be 100% sure who borrowed what because, for example, both Matthew and Luke mention the Virgin birth of Jesus, but Mark does not. Many overlapping events differ in detail, although they do not contradict each other. Hence, this hypothesis is disputed but we would go with it to show that even with this sceptical position, the NT writings are very early and reliable indeed. So what we know is that they both talk about things which do not appear in Mark and which seem very much authentic too.

Virtually all the scholars of the New Testament agree that they used a common written source of information, which goes back to the early 40ies or earlier, only up to 10 years after Jesus died and rose again! This source the academics call "Q".

To recap: the gospels' authors[7] seem to have drawn from accounts which are immediate (oral tradition from Jesus' disciples) or almost immediate (written sayings of disciples) and they are incredibly similar in their rendering of the events, and yet, at the same time, they are independent enough from each other, based on the content they offer, to remove any doubt of any collusion to concoct a story about Christ.

Then enters the Gospel of John. He is one of the original 12 apostles and he writes in the 90ies, but his written material shows all the signs of someone who has personally been in the 20ies and 30ies, witnessed and took part in what was happening[8].

It is very hard to find any historical figure like Jesus from around that time and even hundreds of years later who is so well attested and historically sound. We know and tend to accept a lot of facts about Julius Caesar, which are mentioned nowhere else but only by the historians Suetonius and Plutarch, who wrote after the year 100 AD and is nearly 150 years after Caesar died! In comparison, the historical evidence for Jesus is

---

[7] Those of us who espouse the traditional view know who most likely they are: Levy or Matthew the tax collector (apostle), Mark (son or close coworker of Apostle Peter), Luke (close co-worker of Apostle Paul and John (apostle).
[8] ibid.

superior, even on the basis of the generally accepted consensus (which is debated and eroded in favor of the traditional view). And if the one for Caesar and other historical figures is enough, then for Jesus, it is more than enough.

The more evidence is discovered, the more reliable the Gospels look.[9] The multiple sources of information about Jesus make it easier to sift through the bits, which are obviously accretions (gnostic books of 2nd century AD), and the authentic facts, which most Christians believed from the beginning.

---

[9] https://voice.dts.edu/article/wallace-new-testament-manscript-first-century/

(13) FACT CHECKING

It is widely understood that the persons who wrote the gospels were not eyewitnesses to Jesus' ministry and were not historians as we would define the term today. Rather, they were educated storytellers who used material from both mostly oral and some written sources while at the same time adding in some embellishments and myths at their own discretion. There was no fact checking available (i.e. no contradicting information sources) and no one alive who could testify that any given story was untrue.

RESPONSE

We should bear in mind that only the secular historians reject the direct eyewitness value of the gospels, but even they do not deny it altogether. Many secular researchers agree that there are numerous eyewitness snippets throughout all the gospels. Bart Ehrman thinks that Jesus' birth in the first century, his baptism by John the Baptist, and crucially, His crucifixion are historically true facts and correspond to the early eyewitness accounts.[10] We, though, cannot expect people without faith in the supernatural to agree with Jesus' virgin birth, miracles, and especially His resurrection. This would take a profound change in worldview.

---

[10] https://ehrmanblog.org/did-jesus-exist-my-debate-with-robert-price/ accessed 23 Oct 2017

Of course, the people who wrote the gospels were not modern professional historians. But no one in antiquity could qualify as a modern academic historian by 21 century standards. Like everyone who used to write history back then, the evangelists wrote about things they believed are important and given that they had no material interest to affirm what they said, we don't see why they would make those stories up at all. By preaching and teaching about Christ, they put themselves at odds simultaneously with most Jews of the time and the rest of the Roman Empire.

Herodotus wrote his books to make money. He had to embellish them in order to make them sellable. Josephus wanted to preserve the memory of the Jews and he was free to create whatever he wished as long as it didn't run against the Roman polity. Had he criticized Rome, things would have been different.

The authors of the gospels faced the world head on and their accounts survived in spite of major and bloody opposition. The four gospels were only part of many other (purported) accounts of the life of Jesus. They (John and Luke particularly) were written partially in response to some fake accounts, which run contrary to what the church had widely accepted. Luke clearly says that his motivation to write was the many accounts circulating around (Luke 1:1). The churches worldwide accepted as authentic the accounts of those four gospels because they agreed with the preaching and the memories of the early oral traditions left by the apostles of Christ.

Matthew was an eyewitness, although his authorship is disputed again by secular and liberal scholars. There are good reasons to think that he was the author, though. His name appears on all manuscripts as early as 125 AD[11]. Very few ancient documents have such strong uniformity of evidence. Papias (120 AD) confirms that "Matei the publican" was the author. If Matthew's authorship was disputed, this would have shown in the writing of the early Christian authors like it happens with The Epistle of Hebrews about which Origen (250AD), "Only God knows who wrote" it.

Also, if it wasn't sure that Matthew wrote it and someone wanted to give it an additional credence, they could easily pick someone else from the apostles who is more famous like Nathaniel, for example, and who was well known for his good character and not necessarily a former tax collector. It would not have been so easy because we have records about a church official, who was preaching the right thing but was attributing his sermons to some of the apostles, and this preacher was reprimanded and shamed. The church and most people at the beginning knew who the apostles were, was very strict to preserve the truth, and was quick to identify and excise wrongs like this.

A pointing piece of evidence is that the first name "Matthew" is only ever mentioned by Matthew himself (9:9) whereas Mark and Luke call him "Levi" (most likely his second name).
The secular scholars suggest the date of Matthew's writing around the 80ies or later. Of course, a big problem for them is the predictions of Jesus about Jerusalem and Israel and they are sceptical that He could tell the future in such a way. Should they accept an earlier date, this would pose manifold serious questions about the reality of the prophetic word of God.

---

[11]

http://www.academia.edu/7738059/Author_of_the_Book_of_Matthew_Argument_and_Debate

An early church author Irenaeus (175AD) asserts that Matthew wrote when Peter and Paul were in Rome, which was before they were killed in around 65 BC, so most of the evidence suggests earlier date, probably around mid 50ies and early 60ies. This brings the written account of this gospel even closer to the events it is relating.

Mark was like a son, or perhaps a biological son, of Apostle Peter (1 Peter 5:13). Papias in 120AD confirms that Mark was the author of the second gospel and he merely related what Apostle Peter told him about the life of Jesus with a view that it would be read by the Romans. Interestingly, when Mark talks about Peter, his account is very detailed and lively and yet the later is presented as somewhat less "heroic" and his good sides and achievements are not so well described as with Matthew and Luke. There are more details about him but less emphasis on his "good side". It was written sometime in the 50ies or 60ies also because we know about Luke, who wrote prior to 65AD (he didn't mention Paul's death in that year) and most scholars across the board agree that Luke used Mark's account as he himself admits that he did a research and read many accounts (Luke 1:1,2).

Luke was a friend and close coworker to Paul, who knew the apostles well. There are hundreds of details in his works (the Gospel of Luke and Acts) which have been confirmed with great precision, and maybe he is the first true historian that we know of.[12] Like the authors of the other gospels, he doesn't mention his name in the text, but it is clear that the receivers knew who the author was.

All the gospels were written initially for people the authors knew well and were known well by. That's how the church was constructed and such a close-knit community it was. They didn't write as a first call for public consumption and to the whole

---

[12] Mltchel, William Ramsay, *Lucan and Pauline Studies* (1908)

Roman Empire, but responded to the needs of the people near them.

Luke never mentioned the martyrdom of Paul in 65AD and the persecution of Christians during the reign of Nero, although he was very careful to record disasters like the empire-wide famine (Acts 11:27-30) and also the expelling of the Jews from Rome by the same Emperor (Acts 18:2). He couldn't miss these events unless he completed both his works before they occurred. Therefore, Luke finished his gospel in the early 60ies, latest, and maybe much earlier, in the 50ies. He talks very vividly about the destruction of Jerusalem and this is one major reason for the sceptical secular scholars to put a date on Luke's gospel sometime after this happens in the 70AD. Luke was not an eyewitness of Jesus, but he was a close companion with Paul, who was an apostle vouched for by the original 11 apostles and who was well informed about what Jesus did and said.

John was an eyewitness. His name is in the title of his gospel and there are numerous texts in it showing that it is he who writes. The phrase "the disciple whom Jesus loved" is mentioned 5 times (13:23, 19:26, 20:2, 21:20, 21:24-25). In the end, he identifies this disciple as the author (John 21:24). This disciple is closely associated with Peter in many places, some of which are 18:15-16, 20:2-9, 21:2-23, and elsewhere in the New Testament. John, the Son of Zebedee, is the only good candidate, given that Peter and James were by this time dead. And from the closest circle around Jesus (those He took to the mountain of the Transfiguration), only John, who was likely the closest, or at least amongst the top three, was alive in the 70ies to 90ies when the Gospel was written[13]. The external evidence of Irenaeus and Clement of Alexandria of 2nd century point out at John the Apostle as well. The earliest manuscript of this gospel

---

[13] http://rowanwilliams.archbishopofcanterbury.org/articles.php/1204/an-introduction-to-st-johns-gospel-st-pauls-theological-centre

dates from 120 AD and comes from Egypt. It has John's name on top. If so early and outside Israel, there is already a tradition for the authorship of John, then this is a strong evidence for the case.[14]

---

[14] Ibid

(14) ROMAN BIAS

As mentioned, almost all of the eyewitnesses of Jesus' ministry were dead by the time of the gospel writings, either of natural causes or as a result of the Jewish-Roman war that began in AD 66. The band of Jewish followers of Jesus, led by his brother James, no longer existed. The only Christians remaining were the Romans and other Gentiles who were followers of Paul's concept of Christianity. Consequently, the gospels are told in a manner consistent with Paul's theology and also with an anti-Jewish, pro-Roman bias. One of the best examples of this bias is the exoneration of Pontius Pilate and the condemnation of the Jews for Jesus' death (Matthew 27:24), a fabrication of the first order (and one that has had tragic consequences for Jewish people for the past two millennia). Another is the story of the Roman centurion who was allegedly commended by Jesus for having more faith than anybody else in Israel (Matthew 8:5-13).

RESPONSE

It is very likely, even if we go with the secular dating, that there were many eyewitnesses of Jesus' times still alive when the Synoptic (first three) gospels were written and admittedly fewer when Apostle John wrote his piece. The sacking of Jerusalem wasn't a big factor for the Christian Jews because they were gradually expelled from Jerusalem by their non-Christian counterparts and also, they didn't take part in the revolt against Rome, so they were not counted as enemies of the state. Most likely, their nonparticipation in the war established a rift between them and the other Jews, but potentially, many thousands of Jewish Christians did not disappear overnight, however, many of them and their immediate descendants were alive and well long after 70AD, when Titus razed Jerusalem.

Paul was very influential and the role of the former gentiles, to whom he mostly preached in the first place, would only grow in significance in the early Church, but we should say that there were always Jews who profess Jesus Christ, and this chain has never been broken to this day.
But was Paul "anti-Jewish and pro-Roman"? That is a very strong statement and factually unwarranted.

In Romans 3:1, Paul asks, "What is the advantage that Jews have?" and he answers, "Great." He never ever spares criticism of some of the Jews for their attitude of hate and disbelief in the Gospel but always affirms God's love and how the Church is indebted to them: "If some of the branches were broken off and you, being a wild olive, were grafted in among them and became partaker with them of the rich root of the olive tree, [then] do not be arrogant toward the branches; but if you are arrogant, remember that it is not you who supports the root, but the root supports you" (Romans 11:17,18), and "regarding the gospel, they are enemies for your sake. But as regards election, they are beloved for the sake of their forefathers" (Romans 11:28).
So Paul wasn't at all anti-Jewish. But was he "pro-Roman"? Well, when he confronted Peter for hypocrisy, he said something astonishing.

14 But when I saw that their conduct was not in step with the truth of the gospel, I said to Cephas before them all, "If you, though a Jew, live like a Gentile and not like a Jew, how can you force the Gentiles to live like Jews?"
15 We ourselves are Jews by birth and not Gentile sinners -- (Galatians 2:14-15).

In other words, he was viewing the Christianizing of the Gentiles as making them more Jewish ("to live like Jews") albeit Jewish in Christ and only through Christ. They were grafted on the Jewish vine which is Christ himself. Jesus was a Jew. He said that during His earthly ministry, He is sent to preach to the Jews:

"I was sent only to the lost sheep of the house of Israel." (Matthew 15:24). "Do not go in the way of the Gentiles, and do not enter any city of the Samaritans; but rather go to the lost sheep of the house of Israel." (Matthew 10:5,6).

To the woman from Samaria who met Him by the well, He said: "You worship what you do not know; we [Jews] worship what we know, for salvation is from the Jews." (John 4:22).

God's covenant with Abraham would never be abolished and the Jews are His people and even though some of them love this world (temptations or traditions) more than God and reject Christ, this doesn't mean that God does not care for them: "I ask, then, has God rejected his people? By no means! For I myself am an Israelite, a descendant of Abraham, a member of the tribe of Benjamin." (Romans 11:1).

To pick up small snippets like the case with Pontius Pilate (actually, Jesus clearly told him that he is sinning by letting Him be killed (John 19:11)) and the case with the Roman centurion (yes, Jesus indicated that His Gospel is not just for the Jews but those who have faith in God through Him (Matthew 8:5-13)), and, thus, make an overarching statement ignoring the whole Scripture is grossly unfair.

(15) GROWING FISH

The stories told in the gospels became more impressive as each new gospel was written. In Mark, there is no account of a virgin birth or of a resurrected Jesus interacting with the disciples (other than the ending verses that were added much later). With Luke, the virgin birth is added. With John, the raising of Lazarus is first presented, and Jesus is for the first time equated with God the Father.

Another example is that the temptation of Jesus by the devil grows in significance and details from Mark to Luke to Matthew. These examples reflect a classic illustration of myth-making, such that events are embellished over time to make for a more persuasive story.

Another example of the evolution of Christian writings is as follows:

Matthew 27:46,50:
About three in the afternoon Jesus cried out in a loud voice, "Eli, Eli, lema sabachthani?" (which means "My God, my God, why have you forsaken me?")... And when Jesus had cried out again in a loud voice, he gave up his spirit.

Luke 23:46:
Jesus called out with a loud voice, "Father, into your hands I commit my spirit." When he had said this, he breathed his last.

John 19:30:
When he had received the drink, Jesus said, "It is finished." With that, he bowed his head and gave up his spirit.

In Matthew, Jesus is expressing displeasure with God for allowing the crucifixion, but in the later gospels, Luke and John, there are no longer any hints of dissatisfaction. It suggests that the writers of the gospels made revisions to improve the image of Jesus and to make it appear that he viewed his crucifixion as an expected and necessary part of his earthy mission.

RESPONSE

Mark wrote with a view to present Christ as the Son of God who came to serve. In Mark 2:7, Jesus is directly equated with God by forgiving sins, and, of course, he receives accusations in blaspheming. Although Mark's story is all about action, and "Immediately" appears very often in the text. The other gospel writers dwell much more on what Jesus said (think about the Sermon on the Mount) on the prophecies about Him (numerous quotations) and on the environment in which His ministry unfolded - generally curious, somewhat diverse, and highly adverse.

Often, although shorter as a book, the "Gospel according to Mark" gives more details when he describes Jesus' miracles than the other gospels do when telling the same story. This is so with the healing of the blind man in Capernaum (1:21-27), the healing of many sick and oppressed in the evening (1:32-34), the cleansing of a man with leprosy (1:40-45), the healing of the paralytic lowered down through the roof (2:1-12), etc. Mark doesn't pass on much of Jesus' words but Jesus is the One who can do it all, the Man and God of action.
"They were overwhelmed with amazement. 'He has done everything well,' they said. 'He even makes the deaf hear and the mute speak.'" (Mark 7:37).
There are some things Mark (like John, but for different reasons) wasn't interested in because Mark was focusing on the

actions in ministry. He was presenting Jesus as a minister, problem-solver on Earth and for eternity.

For Matthew, the description of Jesus' physical birth was a must because he tied it with the Old Testament's prophecies, and for Luke, it was important because he wanted from the outset to be very comprehensive and add things which were not known in great detail by his addressee, Theophilus, as he indicates in his opening and, hence, his gospel is the longest.

With regards to the temptation of Christ, if we compare Mark and the rest again, these are totally different styles. Mark marks it out as the beginning of Jesus' ministry and Matthew and Luke wanted to show what the details of this encounter with the devil were.

The resurrection of Lazarus (John 11:1-44) is not significantly beyond what Jesus already did when he resurrected the daughter of Jairus (Mark 5:21-43) or the son of the widow from Nain (Luke 7:11-18). He was able to resurrect dead people by the power of the Father in Him from the beginning, so there is no development of character here. In fact, John has the least number of miracles described and yet, he is the one who writes last. He could have piled up an impressive number of those (we know of 37) but he chooses only 7 miracles, which well illustrates His point that Jesus is the Messiah, the Savior of the world. Clearly, John had different purposes for writing his story and, hence, this reflects on the content, but it's hard to see how Jesus "evolved" from Mark to Matthew to Luke to John as He was essentially the Son of God, sitting on the right hand side of the power/God and the one who has all power in all gospels.

Let's bear in mind that the gospel of John, although written the latest, is the one with possibly the earliest oral tradition. So it's unlikely that John was saying anything new about what Jesus did, but He wanted to present what Jesus was like and help everyone believe in Him and know Him personally.

For Mark, what Jesus did after He was resurrected is not so important because his drift is to show Jesus works, why He did them, and how those who believe in Him can do the same and live a life of God's power manifested through them. Therefore, Mark is about the actions and John is about the person of Jesus.

Matthew and Luke are something in between. The last sayings on the cross of Jesus are several, some of which are mentioned only in one gospel, but the quotation from Psalm 22 ("My God, my God, why have you forsaken me") is both in Mark and Matthew. If anyone wanted to remove it for image's sake, this would have been Mark because he is writing to the Romans and others who may have found it more appealing that Jesus would maybe not die at all but is taken to heaven. They could cut out many other things if this tarnishes His image. Jesus' prayer in Gethsemane garden, Him asking God to "take away this cup," and the angel coming to support Jesus (Luke 22:43) is told to us by Luke, who is supposed to protect Jesus' image of powerful and victorious, and He who never wavered.

Also, in the Gospel of John, Jesus gets tired (John 4:6), which is strange for a divine person.
The truth is that the writers of the gospels and the world have never seen anything like this before - a God-man walking amongst them. Therefore, Jesus is presented in the gospels as both truly God and truly Man, and if they set out to embellish and inflate the story of Jesus, they could have made it up in a whole different manner, but then, Jesus wouldn't have been the unique and holy Son of God and Son of Man.

(16) GOSPEL CONTRADICTIONS

If the scriptures were inspired by God and then accurately copied by scribes, we would expect to see a fairly rigorous consistency among the books. The best way to test this hypothesis is to examine the four gospels, as they all claim to describe the same events. What we see are numerous contradictions, including: The genealogies of Joseph in Matthew and Luke disagree significantly.
Luke has Mary and Joseph traveling from their home in Nazareth in Galilee to Bethlehem in Judea for the birth of Jesus (Luke 2:4). Matthew, in contradiction to Luke, says that it was only after the birth of Jesus that Mary and Joseph resided in Nazareth, and then only because they were afraid to return to Judea (Matthew 2:21-23).

All of the gospels disagree on who found the empty tomb. In Mark, it is Mary Magdalene, Mary the mother of James, and Salome. In Matthew, it is Mary Magdalene and the other Mary. In Luke, it is the women who had come with him out of Galilee, including Mary Magdalene, Joanna, and Mary the mother of James, plus two others. In John, Mary Magdalene found the stone removed and ran back to get Peter and another disciple.

There are also major contradictions about what they saw at the tomb. In Mark, a man in a white robe was sitting in the tomb. In Matthew, an angel was standing on the stone that had been removed. In Luke, it was two men in dazzling apparel. In John, Mary and Peter and the other disciple initially find just an empty tomb. Peter and the other disciple enter the tomb and find only the wrappings. Then Peter and the other disciple leave and Mary looks in the tomb to find two angels in white. After a short conversation with the angels, Mary turns around to find Jesus.

The existence of these and other contradictions can be explained as either (1) the original authors were not divinely inspired and therefore didn't write stories that aligned with each other, (2) scribes made errors in copying the scriptures, or (3) the writings were deliberately revised by scribes to meet their personal biases or beliefs. In any event, it is clear that God was not overseeing the Bible-building effort to ensure a perfect product. As such, the Bible cannot be viewed as a reliable portrayal of history.

RESPONSE

Let us be clear, God inspires the concepts which are important and consequential to the people addressed, but He allows freedom of style, point of view, and vocabulary used by the authors whilst making sure that the message is consistent. The Bible is a very consistent book since it was written by numerous authors, and the gospels are astonishingly complementing each other and provide a solid basis for establishing the facts and claims on which the Christian doctrines rest. We will demonstrate this by going through all examples mentioned above.

The genealogies in Matthew and Luke

The standard demonstrable explanation is that Matthew outlines Joseph's genealogical tree and Luke focuses on Mary's one. Why did they do that? They wanted to show that Jesus is the "son of David" and that He was a descendant of David through both Joseph and His mother, Mary.

Furthermore, in the genealogy of Joseph, as we understand it, there is a problem because God said about Jeconia: "Write this man down as childless, a man who shall not succeed in his days, for none of his offspring shall succeed in sitting on the throne of David and ruling again in Judah" (Jeremiah 22:30). This prophecy is closely fulfilled as nobody from Jeconia's offspring ever sits on the throne of David. The only way the royal line would be continued is if Jesus would come through His mother from a different lineage of David, and yet the original royal line is preserved by Joseph being His adoptive father without a biological connection between Jeconia and Jesus as these genealogies reveal.

Secondly, God said that He will take away the Northern Kingdom from the descendants of Solomon because of his idolatry (1 Kings 11:11).

As we can see, the genealogy of Mary goes through Nathan and not Solomon.

Nazareth and Bethlehem

Luke is more detailed (as with his genealogy) than Matthew, and he explains that Mary is from Nazareth, and Joseph was about to marry her when she found herself with a child. The angel of God told him to take her as wife nonetheless, which he did. They had to travel to Bethlehem, though, due to the need to register for tax purposes as Joseph was originally from there.

Jesus was born in Bethlehem to fulfil the prophecies about His place of birth. It is near Jerusalem, so they could go and sacrifice what is required by the Law of Moses for a first born baby. When Joseph realized that living in Bethlehem is risky due to Herod's son brutal rule, he agreed to settle with his wife and children in her hometown, Nazareth, which would again fulfil another prophecy about Jesus that He would be a Nazarene.

Who found the empty tomb?
We see that Mary Magdalene is there always, and with her, several other people are mentioned. It is most likely that all the people mentioned were there, but again, there is no contradiction because the presence of some does not exclude others. As usual, the different gospels complement each other.

Whom did they see in the tomb or the garden around it?

All accounts agree that they saw angels or "men in a dazzling apparel" who told them that Jesus is alive as He predicted would happen. The details of how it happened could be harmonized but this does not make the point they were making stronger or weaker. To them, Jesus is alive regardless of how it happened and what they saw.

We could think that the events unfolded like this (again, this does not give to or take from the reality of the miracle):

Jesus comes to life as told in the Scripture. The huge rock in front of the tomb is removed by an angel, from whom the soldiers ran away. Then, the women (Mary Magdalene and others) came and looked inside and didn't see anything at first. So Mary Magdalene became upset and went back to tell Peter and the other disciples that the body of Jesus is gone. In the meantime, the other women there saw the angel inside and he told them that Jesus had risen, and they go back to tell everyone. Mary Magdalene returns shortly after and she sees two men who tell her that Jesus is not there and then she turns and saw Jesus Himself, although she didn't recognize Him initially. To John and Matthew, these are angelic beings. To Luke, they are "men in dazzling clothes" (later called "angels"), which again is pointing at angels. And to Mark, this is a man that could have been what the women thought initially.

By all means, it's unfair to expect all details to overlap in every account because that's not what God intended. They surely don't contradict each other, but they are told from different points of view. God allows such frivolity as long as they don't change the theological message because, as we said, God's inspiration does not do away with personal style, point of view, or emphasis.

(17) RAISING OF LAZARUS AND WOMAN CAUGHT IN ADULTERY

The stories of the raising of Lazarus from the dead and the woman caught in adultery are extremely important in the effort to define who Jesus was. One tells of his immense power, and the other tells of his divine wisdom. Both would have been told and retold throughout the region, spread virally, and held up as convincing evidence for having faith in Jesus. However, curiously, neither of these events is documented in the first three gospels (Mark, Matthew, and Luke). Not until the gospel of John, written at least 70 years after the death of Jesus, is the raising of Lazarus documented in scripture. And the story of the woman caught in adultery is not found in the oldest manuscripts of the gospel of John, and only appears in manuscripts beginning in the fifth century. This casts considerable doubt on the historical truth of these events.

RESPONSE

The story about the raising of Lazarus is told only by John. Similarly, the story about the raising of the son of the widow from the town of Nain (Luke 7:11-17) is only mentioned by Luke. Jesus' miracles were numerous and practically impossible to record in their entirety. In the NT, we have about 37 of them recorded, but John tells us that "all the books" may be insufficient to contain all that Jesus did (John 21:25). Also, John relates other stories which we don't see elsewhere, for example, the meeting of Jesus with the woman at the well (John 4:4-26). This doesn't mean anything about their veracity because each author decides which miracle or story they would tell in order to fit their purpose of writing.

None of them had the whole information as well, although the general and most telling facts were known to all of them, which makes the whole narrative stack together well and look truthful. We cannot know every reason why they chose to include some miracles and not others. The discrepancies between the gospels without real factual and, especially, doctrinal contradictions, though, is an evidence that they were telling the truth and nobody would be able to tamper with the texts without this being noticed and corrected.

Regarding the raising of Lazarus, the authors of the Synoptic gospels would have wished to skip this story on the grounds that the Jewish chief priests wanted to kill Lazarus because many Jews were coming to faith in Jesus because of him (John 12:10). By the time John was writing (90-100 AD), Lazarus was most likely dead and the story which was well known by the church could now be "written so that you may believe that Jesus is the Christ, the Son of God, and that by believing, you may have life in his name." (John 20:31).

Regarding the story of the woman caught in adultery, it has been known for thousands of years that its place was not fixed. Mind you, it's never been doubted, as Augustine said some men didn't like it because it may encourage their wives to cheat on them and admittedly it's a bit controversial because it could be abused by someone looking at it through the eyes of the flesh and sin and thinking that they can commit such transgression and it would all be fine in the end. One good explanation proposed by John Burgon (d.1888) a dean of Chichester Cathedral) is that the ancient church skipped this story from the Lectionary (the daily readings from the Bible) because it coincided with Pentecost and they wanted more suitable reading instead of one about adultery and which may be misinterpreted at that. This theory explains why the text is often found at the end of the Gospel of John in some important manuscripts. This theory agrees with the fact that with those very important manuscripts like P66, P75, Codex N, the last page of John's Gospel is missing because it usually wears off as with other codexes. So the absence of the text is not a good reason to think that it is not authentic.

Some medieval manuscripts like "Lambda" skip it, too (if they claim that it was added later, it wouldn't make sense), again, most likely for practical reasons, but they go out of their way to say that this story is found in the most ancient manuscripts! Numerous church luminaries like Augustine, Jerome and others affirmed its authenticity. Textually, it has some 13 words which are unique for John, but that is not a proof that it's not written by John, given that the story was absolutely very unique for the Gospel. Actually, it's a strange way to start a stand-alone text with the sentence, "And everyone went home." When the text is removed, the narrative becomes abrupt, although some say it's exactly the opposite.

No early theologian ever doubted its veracity and it's been found in some manuscripts since mid 200s AD. But even if we admit for the sake of the argument that it's not really written by John, this doesn't change much about the NT doctrine. It changes nothing at all. But it shows how even such story, which other evangelists didn't even mention because, most likely, they didn't find so important, took a great deal of attention from very early times. This, again, proves how diligent and efficient the church and its multi-source manuscript system was in preserving the authenticity of the New Testament.

(18) PALM SUNDAY / GOOD FRIDAY CONFLICT

Jesus is adored and worshipped as a King as he enters Jerusalem on Palm Sunday. He then proceeds to work miracles, heal the sick, and demonstrate his supreme wisdom, making him even more of a figure for adulation. But five days later, without explanation, he is abruptly hated so much by his own people that, given a chance to have him released, they chose to free a common criminal instead. There is something seriously wrong with this story.

What most likely happened is that the account of these events was altered to absolve the Romans and place the blame for Jesus' death on the Jews (see Problem #21). This is because by the time the scriptures were written, the focus of Christian evangelism was on the Gentiles throughout the Roman Empire, while the Jews, freshly defeated in their war with Rome, were viewed as detestable villains.

RESPONSE

Jesus entered Jerusalem and numerous people were greeting Him and praising God for the great works He did through Him. But there were over 500,000 people in the city for the day of Atonement. How many of them were actually admirers of Jesus? 10% - 15%?

Like today, the majority of the Jewish people did not accept Jesus but a significant minority did. Of course, when the Romans intervene and pass a judgement against Him and given His insistence that His disciples shouldn't fight with arms and weapons, you can expect that they would disperse as it happened. Jesus clearly said that the Romans also have committed a sin by doing this even though pressurized by the Jewish leaders, saying, "...bigger sin has the one who handed me over to you" (John 19:11).

The evangelists are very graphic when they describe how brutal the Roman soldiers were with Jesus. The Jewish tetrarch Herod Antipa "despised" Jesus but did not touch Him with a finger. Pilate got Him beaten (the Romans were famous with their harsh ways of corporal punishment), and this turned out to only be preparing Him for the worst - torture and crucifixion. Apart from one slap on the cheek in the house of the high priest, the Jewish people didn't beat Him, but the Roman soldiers were hitting Him and asking, "Who did hit you, guess!"(Matthew 26:68).

Then, what was the attitude of the first church - the one in Jerusalem - and the apostles toward the Jews? They actually kept on living as Jews but were putting their trust in God through Christ for salvation and not in the Law of Moses.

In Acts (written before 70 AD as discussed already), the disciples lived with the Jews and had them as their brothers. They remained in Jerusalem in spite of sporadic persecution which was no bigger than in many other places which were populated by Gentiles.

Peter, in his first sermon, called the Romans "wicked men" (Acts 2:23), and called all people, regardless of their background, to salvation: "For the promise is for you and for your children and for all who are far off, everyone whom the Lord our God calls to himself."

Jesus also says that the "time of the nations trampling Jerusalem " (Luke 21:24) would be ended and Jerusalem would be redeemed by Him.

Similarly, Apostle Paul says: "And in this way all Israel will be saved, as it is written, The Deliverer will come from Zion, he will banish ungodliness from Jacob" (Romans 11:26).

Israel is the only nation, as described in the New Testament, that would be saved in its entirety when Jesus comes, meaning that they would all repent as one and receive their righteous Servant-King. That's hardly a biased anti-Jewish approach.

(19) JUDAS

The story of Judas, the traitor, is fraught with inconsistency. First and foremost, it should be obvious that what he allegedly did actually hastened the salvation of mankind, as defined by Christianity. Without Jesus' capture and execution, everybody would still be subject to the condemnation of original sin as well as their personal sins. Second, Jesus was not in hiding during his time in Jerusalem. He was out and about, performing miracles, and routinely in plain view of the Roman authorities, making it unnecessary for anyone to rat him out for arrest. Third, if we are to believe Christian doctrine, Jesus knew that he was to be executed and that this was the principal point of his mission, so why would he call out Judas as a traitor both at the Last Supper and in the garden at the time of his arrest? Judas actually offered a beneficial contribution to Jesus' mission.

To make some sense of this story, one has to assume that it was changed to fit a new narrative that placed blame on the Jews for the crucifixion. Painting Judas as a traitor was a part of that effort. What probably happened was that Judas was sent by Jesus to entice the Roman soldiers to the Garden of Gethsemane. Jesus then expected that God would miraculously intervene to defeat the Romans and begin the reign of Jesus as the king of the restored Kingdom of Israel.

RESPONSE

Here, the questioner doesn't take into account that God can see what would happen from outside time and make His plan unfold accordingly. God knew that Judas would betray Jesus and, hence, Jesus chose him to be one of the twelve. Jesus said, " Did I not choose you twelve? But one of you is a devil" (John 6:70). If Judas was someone who would have repented and followed Jesus until the end, then he would not have been selected to fill the place of "the son of the perishing."

The NT authors clearly say that Jesus had enough supporters to make His arrest a possibly messy affair. Nobody wanted another uprising. If they arrested Him in broad daylight as He was teaching, with potentially hundreds of people around Him, this could have caused some backlash. But He was arrested in the night when Jesus was with only handful of His disciples. There was still some violence involved, though (Peter cut the ear of a man called Malch (John 18:10)). Such an arrest should have been planned very carefully as they did and they needed someone to let them know when Jesus is most vulnerable and easy to intercept and take into custody.

Judas made a free choice about God, which all of us are capable of. Once a person decides to be forever away from God (on a spiritual level, this, at some point, is an eternal and sad decision), then they could become anything which a villain would do in God's plan. Jesus is not happy that Judas makes this decision and this is how God is: He knows what a man would do but still shows great patience as per His mercy (Romans 9:22).

If Jesus gave a green light to Judas to do this instead of a warning that there is no way back, Judas would not have felt so torn apart with guilt that he actually committed suicide (Matthew 27:3-10. This question is written with no consideration of God being in control of the whole situation in a divine and all-knowing way.

(20) ROMAN CENSUS OF LUKE

The Gospel of Luke states that a Roman census was conducted during the time of Jesus' birth (BC 4). There is no record of this in Roman history. According to the Romans' meticulous records, the only census that took place during this time frame was in AD 6-7 and it did not include the areas of Nazareth and Bethlehem. According to Luke, the residents were required to travel to their cities of birth to be counted. This absurd requirement was never applied to any census that the Romans conducted throughout their empire. This would have involved cases where families would have been split apart going to different cities, and it would have devastated the region's economy. Obviously, the Romans would want to know how many people were living currently in each area rather than how many were born in a certain city.

The reason for this artifice from the writer of this gospel is evident. Jesus was known by many to have been born and raised in Nazareth, but the scriptures said that the savior was to be born in Bethlehem. Therefore, some device was needed to convince followers that Jesus was not born in Nazareth as everyone had assumed, but rather that he had the appropriate credentials of the savior.

As a side note, this deception by the author of Luke provides some evidence that Jesus was a true historical figure, given that a mythical person could just as easily

have been invented who was born and raised in Bethlehem.

The Quirinius census has been for a long time one of the passages in the New Testament thought to be closest to "error" done by Luke, by many scholars. Of course, very good explanations have been offered by many other scholars with high view of the Scripture and today, there is a general divide. Those who do not believe that the Bible is a book inspired by God think it's an example of an error, and those who believe in its Divine inspiration, and think that we should take into account all small details in order to assess Luke's account fairly, and assume that he is right until proving that it's not the case, see no real problem with it. Luke being wrong has never been proven, though. The information is so insufficient that many good evangelical biblical scholars say that despite the good explanations, there is a need for more information from early sources, which will fully vindicate Luke before the skeptics, but that is short of admitting that he is wrong.

Notwithstanding, this Luke is incredibly accurate in his way of recording history in both his books (Gospel of Luke and Acts), and Sir William Ramsay famously said that Luke is correct about 54 cities, 32 countries, 9 islands, and many other details which makes him "first class historian" and maybe "the first real historian."[15]

Archaeological inscriptions show that Acts, for example, contains accurate details of the 1st-century society, specifically with regard to titles of officials, administrative divisions, Empire-wide events and enactments, town assemblies, policies towards public gatherings, and rules of the Jewish temple in Jerusalem. We have records of several censuses carried out

---

[15] http://spu.edu/depts/uc/response/new/2013-spring/bible-theology/jesus-according-to-luke.asp

under Augustus, which tell us that he was keen to get the Empire accountable[16]. When Luke says "the whole universe," this would mean Augustus' state policy, which was that the whole empire has to be registered and pay their taxes. This does not mean one count in one go, but counting of all. Under his rule, we know of at least 3 censuses[17]. The first census we know of was in Italy in 27BC, around when Augustus sat on the emperor's throne. Another was in 8 BC and then one in 14 BC. The one which Luke mentions in Acts 5:37 and which occurred during Quirinus governance proper was in around 6 AD and was the localized Judea-wide count, which, as we said, was part of a bigger state policy under Augustus that was completed in year 14 BC. It may be a stand-alone census at the time, which is reflecting the general policy to count the whole "universe".

It is not strange that an enormous empire comprised of tens of provinces and vassal kingdoms would take some time to complete the counting of its subjects, especially if some of the populace were restless. That last detail was the reason why the second census under Quirinius was mentioned at all by Josephus[18] and Tacitus: It was notorious for the raising up in the revolt of some Jewish people led by Judah the Galilean (Acts 5:38). This explicitly shows that the census around Jesus' birth (4BC) is not the one linked with rebellion and riots.

During the first census, Judea was still a vassal kingdom (later, it lost this status and became a province) meaning that, at the time, it would not be counted as it was usual for the other provinces. The local ruler (Herod the Edomite) in collaboration with Roman officials (Quirinus was most likely an important official but not yet a formal governor) would decide when and how exactly this can be done.

---

[16] https://www.csun.edu/~hcfll004/romancensus.html

[17] Wallace, Sherman Le Roy, Taxation in Egypt from Augustus to Diocletian, PUP

[18] Flavius Josephus, *Antiquities* 20.5.2 10

It could be very much the case that this was one of the series of censuses that we know was happening, but due to their local nature were not all preserved in the records. As we said, the second one was mentioned more widely in connection with a rebellion, which attracted the interest of the historians.

There was a census in 8 BC that could have been closely linked with the one Luke is talking about in the gospel. Luke could have easily placed Jesus' birth in Bethlehem without mentioning Nazareth first as did Matthew but his attention to detail was meticulous. He wanted to tell the truth, as it occurred, "from the beginning."

Joseph was from Bethlehem. He may have thought of relocating because his young wife was from Nazareth, but his lands (the Jews kept careful record of this) were in Bethlehem area and the allure of "home" was so strong that the only reason mentioned in the gospels that he moved to Nazareth permanently was the fear of Herod's son. When the census was announced, he probably had nothing in Nazareth to register but had assets in Bethlehem, so he had to travel there. His wife was pregnant, but he didn't want to leave her, and if he thought to settle back in his hometown, she had to come with him.

Although the story of Luke in need of more data for a full picture is clearly stacking together and even though this is one of Luke's historical accounts which are least independently attested, his level of history recording, in general, is so outstanding that he could be reasonably trusted for this reason alone and also for those who believe in God for His invisible hand guiding Luke.

(21)

The four gospels state that the Roman governor over Judea, Pontius Pilate, was obligated during the Passover to commute one prisoner's death sentence and to have him released based on the acclamation of those attending the ceremony. There are no Roman records suggesting that such a custom existed. Further, the implication of such a practice would be absurd. It would mean that the Jews could plan for someone to perform a heinous crime just before the Passover and then have that perpetrator released.

This fictional story was first added to Mark's gospel and then copied by the writers of the subsequent gospels. The author of Mark used this tale, perhaps inspired by a similar story in Homer's "The Odyssey" to shift blame for the crucifixion away from the Romans and toward the Jews. It is likely that Barabbas (translated as "son of the father"), the name of the criminal allegedly chosen by the crowd for release, was actually a nickname used for Jesus. So, in effect, the crowd was actually demanding the release of Jesus, finding that his arrest was unwarranted. When the author of Mark was confronted with the folklore that the Jews were asking for the release of Barabbas, he simply made Barabbas into a separate individual and then concocted the myth of the prisoner release tradition.

RESPONSE

The Paschal release is something which the evangelists call "Jewish custom" (John 18:39) and "Pilate's custom" (Mark 15:6, Matthew 27:15), but not a Roman one. This appears to have been something which Pilate and the Jews of the time, led by the high priest Kaiafa (who was himself appointed with the help of Pilate), had agreed between themselves. It is very unlikely that Pilate would let any prisoner go, but those who are found guilty, with inconclusive evidence, which Barrabas' most likely was, would have been executed by the time of Passover.

In the Roman legal system, by that time, there was already the principle (Jus Gentum) that the magistrates (Pilate acting as such on this occasion) had the right to "to promulgate edicts in order to support, supplement or correct the existing law."[19] The jurist Gaius (130-180AD), who was very influential in his time, summed up the existing phenomenon like this: "Every people *(populus)* that are governed by statutes and customs *(leges et mores)* observes partly its own peculiar law and partly the common law of all mankind."[20]

Barnabas is called "a notorious prisoner" by Matthew (27:16), "a bandit" by John (18:30) and he was "imprisoned with the rioters" (Mark 15:7), and "a man who had been thrown into prison for a riot started in the city and for murder" (Lk 23:19), which means he was well known, and at the same time, his guilt was mixed up with others and one could not tell if he merited the death penalty.

From the four gospel accounts (they all agree on Barabas being released instead of Jesus); only Luke points at murder, but alongside other people, which speaks of someone who could have been released without making an overly bad example of it, but who, at the same time, had enough on his file to be punished in a way that would teach future rioters a good lesson. Pilate clearly had a choice and the right to exercise it. He was a bit

---

[19] Cf. Berger, Adolf. Encyclopedic Dictionary of Roman Law. The American Philosophical Society. 1953. p 529.

[20] Gaius 1.1; quoted in Laurens Winkel, "The Peace Treaties of Westphalia as an Instance of the Reception of Roman Law", in *Peace Treaties and International Law in European History*, p. 225.

biased because he saw that Jesus committed no real crime or even remotely took part in it, but the possible political clout of His sermons which discussed a different kingdom - the Kingdom of God - insisted that He is King even before Pilate made Him a good candidate for enemy of the state designation and, hence, capital punishment (Pilate said to him, "So you are a king?" Jesus answered, "You say that I am a king. For this purpose I was born and for this purpose I have come into the world—to bear witness to the truth. Everyone who is of the truth listens to my voice." (John 18:37)).

In every case, to this very day, when a judge is being involved (watched Judge Judy?) there is an element of subjectivity, which is within the boundaries of the law and depending on the judge's decision.

Therefore, both cases presented an opportunity for Pilate to exercise his discretion to teach a lesson and also show mercy as a good PR to his subjects. Although he was known as a very harsh ruler sometime, but he knew when he should make a compromise for the sake of peace and tranquility (Luke 13:1), even though he had to be pressed to do it by hinting a disloyalty to the Emperor: "If you let this man go, you are no friend of Caesar. Anyone who claims to be a king opposes Caesar." (John 19:12).

Kaiafa and the other priests and servants of the temple (they were hundreds of them) and some of the people who were around demanded quite logically and convincingly that Jesus is the one to be crucified. Barabas presented no threat but Jesus was eating up from their flock and exposing their bad practices. They forcefully reminded Pilate that what Jesus is saying, even in front of him, about His royalty is effectively a challenge to the Emperor himself. Pilate was pushed into performance mode - he had to prove to everybody that he is loyal to his lord.

Naturally, he agreed to their demands, even though he was warned by Jesus that such miscarriage of justice would be a sin (John 19:11). This was the easier thing to do and the price was not that serious - one rabbi who was hated by nearly all other Jewish leaders.

There is really no good evidence to back up another scenario like the suggestion that Jesus and Barabbas were one and the same person. This is an old and obsolete now idea of some liberal theologians who often make their name by controversial statements and career by trying to show that the Bible is wrong.

If Jesus was a mere rioter and political prisoner, the whole religious establishment would have little motivation to demand His execution and latter on persecute His followers. This would have been the job of the state. But as we see in history, Jesus and the Church has been mostly persecuted by the religious authorities (Jewish and pagan) and then, by extension, the state. It is absurd to say that they actually wanted His release. The priests and servants of the temple were in their majority His biggest foes. They would not have ever demanded that freedom is granted to Him.

This hatred was so intense because Jesus addressed the realm of religion and said that it has to be changed toward a transparent, sincere and true relationship with God. Their vilifying attitude toward the Church, later on, was telling.

In the New Testament, it is clearly shown that both the Jews and Romans are at fault and although the Jews of the time on this occasion had the major role, they were no different than the Romans and all other pagans who persecuted "Jesus' body" (the Christians).

Apostle Peter, in his prayer for more boldness, implicated all power groups in that society:

"For truly in this city there were gathered together against your holy servant Jesus, whom you anointed, both Herod and Pontius Pilate, along with the Gentiles and the peoples of Israel" (Acts 4:27). No one involved had a clear conscience.

(22)

The selection of the gospels to be included in the Bible was made by a council of Christian bishops convened in Nicaea in Bithynia by the Roman Emperor Constantine I in AD 325. At this council, four gospels were selected from a total of approximately 60 that were in use at the time. Three of the four gospels selected are called the Synoptic Gospels: Mark, Matthew, and Luke. These were not independent efforts but had many elements borrowed and shared among them. The fourth gospel, John, is very different from the other three and presents a somewhat contradictory theology.

The other 56 or so gospels that were discarded do not agree for the most part with the four that were selected. Examples are the Gospel of Thomas, the Gospel of Judas, the Gospel of Peter, the Gospel of the Nazarenes, the Gospel of the Ebionites, and the Gospel of the Hebrews.

It is likely that the truth of what happened lies buried amid the numerous tales told by all of these gospels, with various true and fictional elements scattered throughout. But what should be troubling to a questioning believer is that the council undoubtedly preferentially selected the gospels that were favorable to the Romans (i.e., the ones that made them look good) and excluded whatever did not flatter them. It is certain that this process resulted in a whitewashed portrayal of history.

RESPONSE

With the advent of Jesus on earth, the Christian Church was established. Less than 300 years after Jesus' death, resurrection and ascendance, 27 books, which will comprise the New Testament, were largely crystallising as those which are worthy of teaching from and following after. The criteria, which (in retrospect) we can see, guiding the collective consciousness of the Church were:
- Every book had to be traced back to an apostle from the first generation when Jesus was walking on the earth. The apostles or their close co-workers, who were directly approved by them, could be trusted as authentic recorders of the words of Jesus.

- The inspired books had to be accepted universally by the vast majority of the Church.
- They had to bear a consistent message. There could not be a book in the NT canon that disagrees on anything of theological value with the other books. Some apparent factual discrepancies of stories recorded in the gospels are considered a strength because this meant the authors had an independent mind about what would actually be included and they generally agreed about all the major theological points and regarding the most important facts.
- All books had to pass the "test of universal usefulness". They had to be used in liturgy across most of the Church.
Regarding the OT, the ancient Christians readily accepted the Tanakh (the Hebrew Bible) as God's word because Jesus did. "He said to them, 'This is what I told you while I was still with you: Everything must be fulfilled that is written about me in the Law of Moses, the Prophets and the Psalms.'" (Luke 24:44). All His apostles did too. In Acts 2:14-41, apostle Peter was extensively using Scripture in his first sermon, and in 1 Corinthians apostle Paul says: "For what I received I passed on to you as of first importance: that Christ died for our sins according to the Scriptures, 4that He was buried, that He was raised on the third day according to the Scriptures, and that He appeared to Cephas and

then to the Twelve...." thus showing that the first witness about Jesus is the Hebrew Bible and then come Peter, the other apostles, and many others.

We can see that all these criteria of canonicity used by the first Christians leave no real room for any other 'known to us' book to qualify as authentically inspired by God for teaching men His will. There were numerous other books, which different, self-professing and some genuine Jewish and Christian groups accepted as originating from God, but none could stand to the criteria outlined above. Maybe the sheer majority of those noncanonical books are available today for us to see and measure up against those criteria.

We have evidence for about a couple of dozen not "54 rejected 'gospels'". Even if there were more, it doesn't change anything but affirms that the church carefully sifted through, over many years, those books, which match the requirements for canonicity.

There are two categories of rejected books (not just gospels) which I want to give example with: those who were so far fetched from the canonical message that they could be easily discerned as merely human works and those who appeared plausible to at least some of the Christian communities but never became accepted by the majority. Just to confirm, none of those were universally or nearly universally part of the church lore of holy books.

The Gospel of Thomas is a book of 114 alleged "sayings" of Jesus, but only about half of them are consistent with the rest of the approved gospels[21] and some of those sayings are so bizarre that when ancient authors quoted from this "gospel," they were

---

[21] Porter, J. R. (2010). *The Lost Bible*. New York: Metro Books. p. 166.

warning that this book is not reliable, even if there may be good bits in it.

Then there is no evidence by any early church authors that Apostle Thomas wrote a gospel (By the way, it is not a gospel at all as there is no story that is being told but just selected "sayings").
In short, this "gospel" fails all the above criteria. It is not written by a first-generation apostle of Jesus or approved by one, not consistent with the rest of the books of the New Testament, not used in lectionaries in most or all of the Church and had never been universally or nearly universally accepted as inspired by God by most of the Church.

The Shepherd of Hermas was a book about visions and prophecies which is not a gospel, but was highly regarded, and some important canon lists include it. Again, though, it was not universally accepted and read because it contained prescriptions for Christians, which are at odds with the rest of the Scripture (for example, it teaches that it is obligatory for partner whose other half has been adulterous to take them back if they repent)[22], and the author was not someone that the ancient church agreed is close to the first apostles of Jesus Christ[23].
So it fails practically all criteria, too.

One would be astonished to find how few books were befitting the high expectations of the church and how zealous the early Christians were to keep the original stories and sayings of Jesus and His apostles preserved and separated from all others lacking authenticity writings.

---

[22] Chapman, John. "Hermas." The Catholic EncyclopediaVol. 7. New York: Robert Appleton Company, 1910. 27 September 2017
[23] Chapman, John. "Hermas." The Catholic EncyclopediaVol. 7. New York: Robert Appleton Company, 1910. 27 September 2017

(23) TOO MANY MESSIAHS

Most Christians believe that Jesus was a unique figure in his time, a one-of-kind preacher who mesmerized followers with his wisdom and magical acts. This is not true. There were many messiahs at this time including Hezekiah the bandit, Simon of Peraea, Athronges the shepherd boy, and Judas the Galilean. In addition, there were many other preachers and prophets who were gathering followers and preaching a messianic message about the coming of the Kingdom of God. Some advocated a violent overthrow of the Roman occupiers as a prelude to the coming. Others stressed a less violent approach including repentance, prayers, and beseeching of God for deliverance. Added to this list is the most popular preacher of all, John the Baptist. Jesus was possibly a follower of John until John's arrest and execution (as exemplified by the subservient act of submitting himself for baptism), and then he may have assumed leadership of John's movement.

Jesus was just one of many itinerant preachers of his day, and there was nothing particularly unique about him, because all were preaching the same ideas, and almost all of them ended up being crucified for the crime of sedition against the Roman Empire. It is a historical fluke that Christians pray to Jesus instead of John or Simon or Hezekiah.

RESPONSE

Jesus was incomparably different to all other teachers. Let us look objectively at the facts we know about those historical figures and then decide if Jesus was special or not.

What do we know about Hezekiah the Bandit?
He lived around 46 BC and was involved in a violent opposition against the rule of Rome over Judea. He was famous for his swift and brutal raids against "gentile" towns on the Syrian border. The newly appointed by Rome king, Herod, put an end to this and captured Hezekiah and killed him without a trial. Hezekiah is a freedom fighter at best, although his methods were crude, brutal and discriminating against those who are not Jews[24].

Simon of Peraea
He was Herod's Slave who rebelled by putting "a diadem" on his head and people around him started calling him "king". He lashed out against Herod and destroyed his palace in Jericho and many of his possessions and plundered what he could from Herod's other properties.
Herod sent one of his captains, Gratus, with some Roman soldiers against the rebels and although the latter fought "boldly if not skillfully," they were dispersed and Simon escaped for a while until Gratus caught up with him and killed him by cutting his head off[25]. There is one inscription found near the Dead Sea in 2000 called "Gabriel's revelation in which somebody called Simon is mentioned and some scholars think this is the same Simon who was Herod's slave. In it, they found a text which was a command by angel Gabriel to Simon (it is disputed if this is Simon of Perea) to "resurrect" or "show up" on the third day. Some scholars who rashly proposed that it says "resurrect" have largely settled with the others which prefer the word "show up" instead[26]. Based on this, some claim that he was a look-alike of Jesus.
Although this is only one "Messianic" line of few words which are partially faded with uncertain origin and addressee and they

---

[24] A.H.M. Jones, *The Herods of Judaea* (1938)
[25] Flavius Josephus, *Jewish War* 2.57-59 and *Jewish Antiquities* 17.273-277
[26] "The First Jesus?". National Geographic. Retrieved 5 August 2010.

had to be reconstructed and, hence, the dispute over their actual meaning and if it's about Simon of Perea at all is still going on.In what justified way a vindictive former slave is compared to Jesus is hard to really fathom.

Anthronges the Shepherd
He was, as his title says, a shepherd boy alongside his four brothers who rebelled against the Romans and Herod (74-4BC) and "slew some out of the hopes of gain, and others from a mere custom of slaying men."[27]

They were typical partisans who fought against Rome and the power of the day, but at the same time, indulged in the trappings of power with no real vision for Israel.
After some success, they were all invariably defeated by Rome and Herod and most of them were killed, and one brother just surrenders himself in the hope for clemency.

Judas the Galilean
This man was stirred up by the second census under Quirinius (6AD) and urged that no Jew should register and he attacked and burnt the houses of those who did. Josephus credits him for starting the violent movement of Zealots (one of Jesus' disciples was formerly of that movement - Simon the Zealot), who were, ultimately, responsible for the war with Rome, which resulted in the destruction of Jerusalem. Some of his sons or grandsons likely took part in the rebellion, but as Gamaliel noted in Acts 5:36-28, even though "he presented himself as a big man," he was vanquished and his people dispersed[28].

As we can see so far, it is hard to find anything truly Messianic, even by the narrow Jewish standard, that Messiah would be a great political leader. All these people were brute, violent, (some

---

[27] Flavius Josephus, Jewish Antiquities 17.278-284
[28] Flavius Josephus, *Antiquities* 20.5.2 102

of them) easily trapped by the indulgences of power and were ultimately defeated in such a way that they left nothing lasting more than several decades (Judas Galilean) and it all came to an end without the enduring influence for Israel, let alone the spiritual state and future of the world.

There is no basis of comparison with Jesus, who rejected violence, refused to be appointed a king, healed and delivered those oppressed instead of killing anyone, and who through death and resurrection, which was convincing enough for His followers, changed the world and it is so to this day.

How about John the Baptist?

He clearly said that he is not Christ (John 1:20) but he was sent to baptise so Christ can be revealed to Israel. He achieved a great spiritual status but his ministry was to lead people to Christ. He himself said, "I need to be baptized by you" (Matthew 3:14) to Jesus, meaning that he needed to be fully baptized with the Holy Spirit which only happens to those who realized that Jesus cleansed their sins, came back to life and lives forever, and then they repent toward God. John is credited with no miracle and actually, it is said: "he did no miracle" but "all that he was saying about Jesus was true" (John 10:41). There is no historical record claiming that John the Baptist had any higher view about himself apart from the revealed in the gospels.

We see that Jesus was indeed a unique teacher and prophet and the nature of His message of love, peace and trust in God have succeeded against all odds where violence and rebellion could not. This shows the divine power of His teaching and actions.

(24) TWO GOSPELS

Unbeknownst to most Christians, the early Christian church had two distinct divisions or denominations. One was organized by the Jewish followers of Jesus, his disciples, and close associates. The other was headed by Paul and his mostly non-Jewish followers.

The Jewish followers of Jesus were led by Jesus' brother James. This group did not view Jesus as being divine, which would be unquestionably contrary to the Jewish faith, but rather a prophet setting the stage for the coming of the new kingdom of Israel to be established on Earth. As mentioned earlier, they viewed the empty tomb as evidence that God has resurrected Jesus into Heaven. But before that, they were certainly disillusioned by the crucifixion because it was not an expected outcome of Jesus' mission. After all, Jesus had just been defeated by the very forces he intended to overcome. It is also likely that Jesus himself did not expect to be put to death. His complaint to God for being abandoned as recorded in the gospel of Matthew (27:46) is probably one of the few Biblical statements by Jesus that can be assumed true because of its disparity with the main gospel message.

With the belief in a resurrection, Jesus' closest followers were refocused to continue to follow his gospel and to expect a quick fulfillment. They were based in Jerusalem and had some success in recruiting new followers for several decades after the crucifixion.

In contrast, Paul viewed Jesus as being both a human and the divine savior of all mankind. Instead of the Jewish concept of a human messiah reigning over a restored kingdom of Israel, Paul envisioned a heavenly kingdom that was open to all peoples with admittance predicated simply on accepting Jesus as a personal savior, and without any obligation to perform good works.

For obvious reasons, a conflict developed between Paul and the original apostles, which shows up the book of Acts and Galatians. When Jerusalem was destroyed by the Romans in 70 AD, the Jewish Christians in Jerusalem were decimated. This eliminated the opposition to the gospel of Paul, which then became the template for the new religion of Christianity. The New Testament books were written by followers of Paul after the destruction of Jerusalem. They were fashioned to support this new gospel, including statements added to make it appear that Jesus saw himself in the role as envisioned by Paul.

In summary, Jesus was a failed prophet, as was ultimately well understood by the Jews. Paul reversed the Jewish theology by viewing Jesus as a God-man and viewing his death as a final sacrifice for the propitiation of sins, making unnecessary any further animal sacrifices that were standard rituals in the Jewish temples.

These events explain the historical irony of how a Jewish preacher became the cornerstone of a new religion that was rejected by the Jews themselves.

RESPONSE

Indeed, two different groups have formed over time in the Church - one of Messianic Jews, who in many ways remained culturally Jewish (they view the sacrifices in the temple not as a way to be forgiven but as a way to remind them and witness about the true sacrifice of Jesus), but put their trust for salvation in Jesus and kept His words; and one which was of gentile origin, who didn't follow the rules and regulations of the Law of Moses, but trusted in Christ for salvation and kept the words of

Jesus and the Old Testament without going into the formality of the rituals.

Both groups come from different cultural traditions but find their hope and fulfilling life in Christ.

Apostle Paul who preached to the second group was a Jew and kept the Law's regulations but he never allowed anyone to believe (as did Peter, the leader in Jerusalem) that salvation comes through anything else but faith in the love, faithfulness and power of God demonstrated by the death and resurrection of Jesus.

Apostle Paul says that those first apostles "did not add anything to the Gospel I was preaching" (Galatians 2:6).

There is no reason to think that Paul thought that Jesus is God as well as a man, but the rest of the apostles did not believe that. They met on several occasions and their doctrines were very much in harmony. Apostle Peter even said at one point that the writings of Paul are on par with the rest of the Scripture (2 Peter 3:16).

Thomas called Jesus "God" (John 20:28); John wrote a whole gospel to show that Jesus is the Divine Son of God, the eternal Word of God (John 1:1-10). Stephen, the first martyr, prayed to "Lord Jesus" to receive his spirit whilst being stoned to death (Acts 7:59); Peter spoke about the transfiguration he witnessed on "the holy mountain" (2 Peter 1:18); throughout all the gospels,[29] Jesus is called "Lord," which is a title only belonging to God.

The gospels would have looked very different if they were written with the mind of complying with the purported apostle Paul's views and emphases in teaching. If they wanted to please

---

[29] The gospels, we can see, were very honestly written because if they were tampered or designed to comply with Paul's or anyone's ideas they would spare some details as Matthew 27:46 mentioned above, but they did not; why would you write deliberately to push your views through and not skip stuff which may be "embarrassing"?

Paul, then the Gentiles, for example, who are mentioned only sporadically and always in some connection with Israel (the chosen people of God), but were Paul's life mission would have had a much more prominent role. Apostle Paul himself expressed a growing frustration with most of the Jews and at some point, he said, "I glorify my ministry (to the Gentiles) (Romans 11:13), yet in the gospels the non Jews are compared to "dogs" (Matthew 15:26), told that they are "worshipping what they don't know" (John 4:22). Jesus even "needed" some convincing in order to help and heal them. The elders had to lobby about the centurion's servant to be healed and the Syrophoenician woman had to argue her way and agreeing that even she may be like a "dog" to the Jews, she also can feed on the crumbs off the children's table.

At the same time, Jesus clearly showed that the Kingdom of God belongs to the non Jews as well (Luke 13:29).
And we see how the two groups converged beautifully at the first Church Council in Jerusalem and that the Gentiles were in the end expected to keep the moral law of Moses but not the regulations and ritualistic rules, but the Jews kept all, not to be saved through it, but to remind and witness about the Saviour of the world - God in Jesus Christ. Both groups affirmed that "we would be saved through the grace of our Lord Jesus Christ" (Acts 15:11).

(25) EVOLUTION DEMARCATION

For those Christians who accept evolution, there is a noteworthy problem dealing with the starting point when humans first became bound for eternity in the eyes of God: There has to be a starting point when God first awarded an eternal life to human beings. Without this demarcation, we would have single-celled life forms living for eternity in heaven. Whenever this occurred, it would create a problem. It would mean that many people going to heaven would do so without the company of their parents, who would die and not be raised up, similar to all of the other animals. No matter where the cut was made, this problem was unavoidable.

RESPONSE

Without defending evolution, it is the opinion of many Christian scholars (William Lane Craig) that it can work well with the Biblical account in spite of its significant explanatory deficiency (personal opinion). If we assume that God, at some point, made the primate "living soul" and "in His image," then there is no point talking about the parents of the first man and woman as they were merely animals without mind, conscience, will, and feelings the way humans do. Animals are driven by instincts and they have no moral obligations or accountability. Human parents care for their children all their life but for animals, after the "child" is grown enough, it is cast out to fend for itself, and if they suffer, the parent would not come to their rescue. For animals, there is a biological relation but not a moral and spiritual one. There is nothing in the Bible about animals going to heaven or hell after they die. For humans, it is the case because humans exist as intelligent beings forever. Humans are accountable for their actions and they are able to make themselves accountable, something we do not see with animals.

(26) TINY DRAMA/HUGE STAGE

At the time the Bible was written, most people viewed the Earth as the center of the universe while the sun, stars, planets, and moon revolved around its flat surface. Christianity is based on this worldview, placing an emphasis on humans as the ultimate reason that the universe was created in the first place. Not only is Christianity Earth-centered, but it was also limited to a few hundred square miles in its beginning and did not reach all areas of the Earth until about 1,500 years later. Further, it is limited in its overall time scope to something less than 10,000 years.

What we have since learned about the age and size of the universe has spectacularly dwarfed the Christian world view. Instead of being 10,000 years old, the universe is approximately 13,800,000,000 years old. Instead of the Earth and a few objects orbiting around it, we have the Earth (4,540,000,000 years old) orbiting the sun, which is just one of about 300,000,000,000 stars in the Milky Way galaxy, which itself is only one of at least 176,000,000,000 galaxies in the observable universe.

The idea that all of this was created so that God could create and test human beings is absurd. If that was so, then:

Why did God wait more than 9,200,000,000 years after creating the universe to construct the Earth? Why did God wait 4,500,000,000 years after creating

the Earth to create human beings?
Why did God wait 100,000 years after creating modern human beings before making any contact with them?
Why did God allow 3,500 years to pass after the initial contact with humans was made before his Word had spread world-wide?
If God is a perfect creator and designer, why is the universe so chaotic, disordered, and messy?
These thoughts are best summed up by a quotation from Richard Feynman:

"It doesn't seem to me that this fantastically marvelous universe, this tremendous range of time and space and different kinds of animals, and all the different planets, and all these atoms with all their motions, and so on, all this complicated thing can merely be a stage so that God can watch human beings struggle for good and evil — which is the view that religion has. The stage is too big for the drama."

RESPONSE

The material creation or the universe is a "stage," which, if read correctly, would get one to know God better.
We should be clear that nowhere in the Bible does it say that the earth is the center of the universe. Some verses are quoted as, "The sun rises and the sun sets, and hurries back to where it rises" (Ecclesiastes 1:5) to argue that this means that the Sun is the active part in relation to the Earth than the other way round, but this is not what the Bible claims. This is a phrase which is used based on how it appears to the author. He was not discussing cosmology. Many of us would express it in the same way today, although we never mean geocentrism. Similarly with other verses, which are read as if they bear on cosmology when they are meaning theological and philosophical truths.

It is true that the Catholic Church in the past had adopted the view of geocentrism, linking it with the importance which humans have for God but this is not what the Bible says. The people who proved that geocentrism is wrong and that the earth is not static (Copernicus and Galileo) were both Catholic Christians.

Similarly with the notion of a flat earth. If the Bible says, "four corners of the earth" (Revelation 7:1; 20:8), this doesn't mean four physical "corners," but the four geographical directions - south, north, east, and west.

God created humans in His image for Himself and He set them on earth with the intention that they can get to know Him. "His purpose was for the nations to seek after God and perhaps feel their way toward him and find him--though he is not far from any one of us" (Acts 17:27).

What about the issue of the vastness of space and time?

The universe appears so vast and humans so small and insignificant in material terms that, actually, it is the perfect stage to show the greatness of the love of God. He considers us so important, even though in the context of the material universe, we are "less than nothing."

"All the nations are as nothing before Him, they are accounted by him as less than nothing and emptiness" (Isaiah 40:17).

In terms of time - 13.5 billion years[30] - any of us or all of us are just like a speck of dust— practically nothing.

In terms of space (billions of galaxies), our life on earth individually and the existence of all nations is like nothing.

In terms of what the whole material universe is as material value - zero - the universe is nothing itself and the nations, of course, are "less than nothing.

But in terms of the love of God: we are "so loved that God gave His only begotten Son that everyone who believes in Him would have eternal (opposite of nothing) life" (John 3:16).

---

[30] http://w.astro.berkeley.edu/~dperley/univage/univage.html

Furthermore, the chaos and disorder are only in relation to human life in most of the universe bar the earth where God created the conditions for life to exist. The universe is governed by laws and the earth being a rare, small dot where intelligent life can exist only raises the stake of the evidence for a Creator.

God has never stopped giving humans messages and His word, but in the end times, He sent His Son for their salvation. The humans who have lived after Jesus comprise over 90% of those who ever lived[31]. God's timing is always right and He never left humanity without an option to know Him. The stage is vast but the Creator's plan is even greater indeed.

---

[31] http://www.worldometers.info/world-population/world-population-by-year/

(27) CHOSEN PEOPLE

Christians are obligated to accept the fact that God first chose to minister and support only the Jews, and to ignore all others, and even to assist the Jews in plundering the neighboring Gentile populations. At the time there were large civilizations in Asia, Europe, North and South America, Africa, and Australia. People living in these areas did not learn anything about Jesus until centuries later, some even until around 1,500 years later. To consider this fact is sobering. Why would God do this, ignore humans for tens of thousands of years only to present himself solely to a desert tribe on a tiny spot of land? A more reasonable explanation is that the Jewish people invented a God that favored them, just like nearly every other culture that has ever existed.

RESPONSE

Indeed, the Scripture says that God chose Israel to reveal Himself to them as a nation in an unprecedented way. We assume that this happens sometime in the 1200s BC when Moses led the people of Israel to Canaan. The whole population of the Earth was about 50 million[32] and God says clearly through Moses that He chose the Israelites, even though they were "the smallest of all people":

"It was not because you were more in number than any other people that Yahweh set his love on you and chose you, for you were the fewest of all people" (Deuteronomy 7:7).

---

[32] http://www.worldometers.info/world-population/world-population-by-year/

"...because He promised so to their forebear Abraham..." (Deuteronomy 7:8).

So, ultimately, it all goes down to the individual's response to God's call. Abraham was not the only person who spoke with God or had visions or was given directions from God for his good.

It seems, upon reading the OT carefully, that God was revealing Himself to individual people from different tribes and origins all the time and not just to Abraham or his descendants.

Let us look at two examples: Melchizedek and Balaam.

In Genesis 14:18-20, Abram is met after his victorious battle by the king of Salem (later Jerusalem) with bread and wine and Abram gave him a tenth of all bounty. This king is called "priest of most high God" and it is said that he was bigger than Abraham himself spiritually because Abraham was blessed by him and not the other way around (Hebrews 7:7). Furthermore, giving him a tenth "of all" is the ultimate honour shown to a spiritual man. So here, we see someone who is not of the biological progeny of Abraham or Israel who was a priest of God and a towering spiritual figure.

Another example of a person who could hear the voice of God was prophet Balaam whose life sadly ended very badly due to his greed.

He was hired to curse the Israelites by the king of the Moabites Balak but God gave him three times blessings instead of curses. It is clear that God was talking to this man even though he was not Israelite. God has His ways of getting to those who want to listen and He would judge everyone righteously. In some ways, every human being had some revelation of God and "none has any excuse" (Romans 1:20) to reject Him.

God is choosing people though who would get to know Him closer and then would be able to reach others with the full message of the good news of His love. For God, there is no problem at all to reveal to 50 million or 7 billion souls their need to know Him. We noted in the previous chapter that His Son, the eternal Word, came on earth when over 90% of the people were about to be born in the future so His ultimate revelation, as far as numbers are concerned, Jesus - walking as man on the earth - was given in the very dawn of the human existence.

(28) IGNORED SCRIPTURES

Some Christians are aware of the absurd laws that are described in the Old Testament, such as being sentenced to death if you work on the Sabbath, or for children to be killed for cursing their parents. They usually say that the Old Testament has been superseded by the New Testament and therefore no longer applies. This is despite the fact Jesus emphatically said the opposite.

"Do not think that I came to abolish the Law or the Prophets; I did not come to abolish but to fulfill. For truly I say to you, until heaven and earth pass away, not the smallest letter or stroke shall pass from the Law until all is accomplished. Whoever then annuls one of the least of these commandments, and teaches others to do the same, shall be called least in the kingdom of heaven; but whoever keeps and teaches them, he shall be called great in the kingdom of heaven." (Matthew 5:17-19)

But to be generous, let's look strictly at the New Testament. What we find are many scriptures even there that are completely ignored by Christians, such as the following:

Luke 6:29-30:

"If someone slaps you on one cheek, turn to them the other also. If someone takes your coat, do not withhold your shirt from them. Give to everyone who asks you, and if anyone takes what belongs to you, do not demand it back."

Matthew 5:32:

"But I tell you that anyone who divorces his wife, except for sexual immorality, makes her the victim of adultery, and anyone who marries a divorced woman commits adultery."

James 5:14:

"Is anyone among you sick? Let them call the elders of the church to pray over them and anoint them with oil in the name of the Lord."

Matthew 6:19:

"Do not store up for yourselves treasures on earth, where moths and vermin destroy, and where thieves break in and steal."

1 Corinthians 14:34:

Women should remain silent in the churches. They are not allowed to speak, but must be in submission, as the law says.

Luke 14:12-14:

Then Jesus said to his host, "When you give a luncheon or dinner, do not invite your friends, your brothers or sisters, your relatives, or your rich neighbors; if you do, they may invite you back and so you will be repaid. But when you give a banquet, invite the poor, the crippled, the lame, the blind, and you will be blessed. Although they cannot repay you, you will be repaid at

the resurrection of the righteous."
It goes without saying that a Christian has no authority to pick and choose which scriptures he will follow; either they all apply or none of them do.

RESPONSE

God's Law is the perfect revelation for the receiver. To the Israelites, God gave a Law which could get them into His promise. They kept it piecemeal and for this, they had some troubles, but as we can see, after all that they did and did not do right, today, they are in the land promised to Abraham in spite of many shortcomings. God is the faithful One.

The case of the man gathering sticks on Sabbath and, thence, sentenced to death should be looked at from the point of view of Ancient Israel. This was a day of solemn rest when no one was working including the guards, so him working was committing of national treason and endangering the lives of many as the enemies, for example, could be alerted and attack the Israelites.

The Sabbath had to be kept by all if it was going to be for blessings and not bring hardship.

Similarly, cursing one's parents could endanger the very social fabric of the society. The children had to show respect, even when they disagree with their parents. The elderly ones had to be cared for rather than like with other nations, where they were left to die more quickly.

What is so difficult about the NT verses mentioned?

Luke 6:29-30

Jesus talks about the attitude to avoid clashes and seek your own interest at any cost. It is better to turn the other cheek than go to war, which could cost you much more. This doesn't mean one shouldn't defend themselves. This means that one should seek a peaceful solution as much as possible.

Jesus and Apostle Paul were both either hit (Jesus) or about to be slapped (Paul) on the cheek and Jesus just said, "Why do you beat me if I haven't said anything bad?" Paul, in turn, said, "You are sitting here to judge me by the Law and against the Law, you tell people to hit me."

Their response was not to abstain from standing up for themselves or what is right and good, but they were simultaneously looking for peace rather than provoke further violence.

That's why Paul says, "If it is possible, as far as it depends on you, live at peace with everyone" (Romans 12:18). That's the point Jesus is making with this admonition - "Be radical about seeking peace and peaceful solution if possible with other people even if they are bad."

Matthew 5:32

Here, Jesus is showing how sacred and holy marriage is. One should not leave their spouse unless they betrayed the covenant between each other by adultery. And if someone leaves their partner for any other reason but adulterous behaviour, then, even though separated, they still belong to each other. If someone marries or has sex with them, that would be adulterous.

The only way a marriage covenant before God can cease to exist is adultery or death. God is serious about marriage, even though people often are not. God's high standard doesn't change, though, and we are challenged to look up to it and by His grace, keep it.

James 5:14

This verse points at the opportunity that every believer has to require the elders of the church to pray for him and anoint him if he is sick. He could confess his sins to them and be assured that through Jesus' intercession, they are forgiven.

On the basis of Jesus' work for the believer on the cross and at the right side of God, the elders ask God for healing with faith.

There is immense power in a prayer with faith and devotion. Many people receive healing this way. This doesn't preclude the believer to seek medical help, though, but often, the medical assessment may confirm the healing which has occurred.

Matthew 6:19:

Jesus says that our treasure should be in heaven. We cannot commit our lives to pursue the desires of the flesh, the vanity of life, and the lures of the eyes because this is not what God has created us for and planned for us. Indeed, He is blessing us with every blessing in heavenly places and being well off is not a vice or sin but material wealth is too low a goal one can aim for.
Jesus doesn't say, "Don't be rich materially," but he says, "Be rich spiritually and make this a priority in your life."

1 Corinthians 14:34:

This is my view, but here, Apostle Paul is saying that women should respect their husbands. There was a tendency that women wanted to dominate their spouses, which Apostle Paul put in the right perspective and order. We know that there were women amongst the apostles (Junia mentioned in Romans 16:7) and this means that given their office of establishing churches and seeing them grow into healthy communities, they had to preach and teach in the church.

Luke 14:12-14:

Here, Jesus does not say that one shouldn't throw a party for their friends or relatives and neither does he say that one should not accept an invitation for a party or feast. Rather, he says that one should feed the hungry and care for those who are despised by others. In this sense, He, in a way, abolished the social classes, and in the church, there were even popes i.e. bishops of Rome who were slaves at the same time.

The words of Jesus should be taken in an attitude of great respect and then their meaning becomes clearer.

(29) JEWISH FATE

If God chose the Jews as his chosen people (a fact necessary for Christianity to be authentic), why did they suffer so many defeats and tribulations at the hands of their enemies? The outcome of many of these conflicts would make it appear that God had chosen the other side instead. This is best exemplified by the Jewish-Roman war of AD 66-73, where the Romans slaughtered the Jews all of the way from Jerusalem to the final stronghold of Masada. It makes no sense that the people backed by an all-powerful God would fall victim to its non-God-aided enemies, much less in such a brutal and convincing fashion.

RESPONSE

The Jews were explicitly warned that they will have to be careful to remember the words of God and keep them, which would have guaranteed that they would succeed in everything they do. In the history of Israel, God's warning has been manifested to be true on numerous occasions. When they were careful to follow what God said, they would make strides. When that was not the case, they would have less of a success or experience big failure. And yet, God had promised them that he would save the whole nation of Israel.

It is true that they, alongside the Romans, crucified their Lord and, thus, they fell victim of the brutality and power of an empire which was immensely mightier than the Jews were and Jesus had warned them about this. The grace of God prevailed, though. Exactly as God speaks about them in the Scripture, He would restore them in their land because His grace, goodness, faithfulness, and love towards them is unending.

They wandered the earth for 2000 years without their own country, endured a grievous and numerous attempts to exterminate them over the course of history, now they are experiencing almost insurmountable opposition to dwell in their own land peacefully and there were and are so many other significant odds stacked against them, but it cannot prevent the promise of God to unfold for them. There is no other nation that would be put back, after such a long hiatus out of their land, in the place where Abraham, Isaak, and Jacob strolled about 4000 years ago.

(30) PRAYER

Objective studies have revealed that prayers are not effective beyond any statistical measure of coincidence. Most notably, they do not work for amputees or paralyzed individuals. Prayers for terminally ill people almost always fail. Prayers for rain, to allay storms, and for fixing damaged property, among others are rarely attempted because the supplicants know they won't be effective. But what do the scriptures say?

Matthew 17:20:

He replied, "Because you have so little faith. Truly I tell you, if you have faith as small as a mustard seed, you can say to this mountain, 'Move from here to there,' and it will move. Nothing will be impossible for you." An objective person must realize that the promise described in this scripture is not true. The fact that there is no discernible efficacy for prayers is a valid clue that there is no God listening and responding to them.

RESPONSE

There is only one relatively large study of the effects of prayers carried out in 2006 called STEP (Study of the Therapeutic Effects of Intercessory Prayer). The participants were 1802 patients who were about to have or had bypass surgery. What was found out was that there was no significant improvement for those who received prayer as opposing to those who didn't. Only the first names and last initial for those receiving prayer were provided to the praying people (no photographs were supplied) and the members of three churches were asked to pray for them.

This study did not take into account the several conditions of effective prayer, though, which are:

It has to be from the heart and out of heartfelt sympathy; providing merely a first name and initial of someone who is otherwise unknown makes it hard for the praying person to put their heart into it.

It helps if the person who is prayed for had asked for it and believe in its efficacy; it turned out that some patients who were told they are getting prayer actually had slightly slower recovery time, most likely due to being "worried" that because they were prayed for, they are probably in a worse state than they thought. They did not believe that it is always beneficial, but instead, they focused on the negative possible meaning that it may have signified. Jesus said, "There were many in Israel with leprosy in the time of Elisha the prophet, yet not one of them was cleansed—only Naaman the Syrian." (Luke 4:27). This would mean that those who seek God, in some way, are mostly those who receive, but, of course, God shows mercy to many who do not necessarily seek Him.

The main motivation and driver for prayer should be the work of the Holy Spirit in the hearts of at least one of the two parties or both and they should go for it out of this kind of personal good disposition for it and not just being told it is happening because someone unbeknownst to them wants to "test" it if it works.

Scripture says: "Do not put the Lord your God to the test" (Deuteronomy 6:16). We can examine the end results of God's work but not try and control its outcome as it happens with scientific tests which create the environment in which they expect God to act.

On another hand, we have numerous testimonies of answered prayers and one case from our church reminds me of its efficacy. A member of our church had punctured aorta, followed by stroke and then perforation of the bowel. His aorta condition was misdiagnosed initially and he was almost sent home, which meant almost sure lethal outcome should that have happened. With the other problems, his lifelong smoking, overweight issues, and age (56), on top of his negative view about many things in life, including saying things like, "God turned His back on us" sometimes, he was very unlikely to recover well, if at all survive in the first place. Yet, many of us prayed for him and he recuperated marvellously and now he is coming back home!

There are quite a few studies which show that people who regularly go to church fare better in many ways than the average. They have a 30 percent reduction in depression, a five-fold reduction in the likelihood of suicide, and a 33 percent reduction in mortality, a study found over 16 years of follow-up.

"The researchers analysed data from questionnaires completed every four years from 1996 to 2012. Among 74,534 women who responded, 14,158 said they attended religious services more than once per week, 30,401 attended once per week, 12,103 attended less than once per week, and 17,872 never attended. Over 16 years, there were 13,537 deaths, including 2,721 from cardiovascular disease and 4,479 from cancer. When the researchers matched deaths with reported religious attendance, they found that women who attended religious services more than once per week had a 33% lower risk of dying during the 16 years of follow-up compared with women who never attended religious services. Women who attended services weekly had a 26% lower risk, and those who attended services less than weekly had a 13% lower risk. The researchers also found that women who went to services regularly had lower rates of smoking and depression and were more likely to have strong social support than those who didn't."[33][34]

In church, there are a lot of prayers, preaching of the Word of love, hope and salvation, and worship, which all are of real beneficence. There are cases reported in the mainstream media of truly paralysed people who received healing. There are numerous reports of very ill people being healed.[35] Actually, what amazed me in the past is that in nearly every charismatic church, you can meet someone who received a miracle.

Jesus is the same, yesterday, today and forever.

---

[33] https://www.health.harvard.edu/mind-and-mood/attending-religious-services-linked-to-longer-lives-study-shows

[34] This is example of following without controlling or deliberately creating environment which is an object to research which seems to fit with the warning of Deuteronomy 6:16

[35] http://www.dailymail.co.uk/news/article-1340497/I-walked-walked-I-felt-like-I-entered-realm-Woman-paralysed-23-years-ago-cured-British-spiritual-healer.html

(31) SLAVERY

The Bible condones slavery. Some Christians today claim that the Bible actually refers to servants, who were presumably working voluntarily for wages. The following scriptures demonstrate otherwise:

Exodus 21:20-21:

"Anyone who beats their male or female slave with a rod must be punished if the slave dies as a direct result, but they are not to be punished if the slave recovers after a day or two, since the slave is their property."

Leviticus 25:44-46:

"Your male and female slaves are to come from the nations around you; from them you may buy slaves. You may also buy some of the temporary residents living among you and members of their clans born in your country, and they will become your property. You can bequeath them to your children as inherited property and can make them slaves for life, but you must not rule over your fellow Israelites ruthlessly." Either the persons who wrote these scriptures were not inspired by God, or God is not good and should not be worshipped. If the former is true, it still must be noted that God did not intervene to remove these verses from the Bible. A real God would have known that slavery is morally wrong and that it would eventually be outlawed through most of the world; for this reason, he would have prohibited slavery to be practiced by his

chosen people.

RESPONSE

Slavery in the ancient world and in the Bible was a social institution. No peaceful person in the Bible could be forced to become a slave and actually abducting someone and enslaving them carried the death penalty in Israel.
If one has lost their ability, though, they could sell themselves as slaves to take care of themselves. This, in Israel, unlike any other country, had a fixed maximum term of 6-7 years. The slave had to be released sometime in the 7th year. It was a serious sin if the owner would not follow the rules of release.
People from another nation could simply accept to be part of Israel by accepting Yahweh as their God and practice the Law of Moses, and they would become eligible for freedom in the seventh year.
"One Law you should have for foreigner and Israelite" (Leviticus 24:22).
Why did God not simply ban the institution right away?
The Law was perfect for the imperfect state of the Israelites. It teaches them important principles, which are valid for all time by specific rules and were applicable to their cultural setting. For example, with divorce, for any reason, Jesus says that although it is allowed under Moses (Deuteronomy 24:1), it is wrong to do it. Jesus said: "Because of your hardness of heart Moses wrote to you this: but I tell you it was not thus in the beginning" (Matthew 19:8). This is because humans were made righteous by God and the coupling between Adam and Eve is the example of that high standard. Marriage was a covenant which they were not supposed to break unless adultery (breaking) is involved (Matthew 5:32).
Also, another example, with animal sacrifice, which they were prescribed to do and which comprised about a third of the Law, God, on many occasions, showed that it's not the kind of

sacrifice He actually wants, but He values the right state of the heart and the eternal sacrifice of Jesus for the sin of the world which it represents (Hosea 6:6).

Similarly, as with those examples where God gives them rules which lead them in the right direction but are not the end point, with slavery, God knew that they wouldn't listen if He told them to abolish it right away, but He mitigated it a great deal and set them on a road to practical slavery (as they knew it) abolition.

In resume, the slaves:

Could not be forced into slavery
Should be released each 7th and 50th year whichever sooner
Shouldn't be treated harshly
If beaten this could be a cause to release them early for a broken tooth, for example, which undoubtedly prompted the masters to be more careful and less harsh
If they are a foreigner (bought or taken during war), they would be released in year 50 (which may be only a few years or even months away) or on the 7th year, if they accept to worship God and follow the Law of Moses

This must have radically changed the culture about slaves by introducing the notion of the importance of sure release after certain time, something which was unheard of.

What are the lessons we learn from the institution of slavery in ancient Israel?

Freedom is precious - protect it, don't become a slave easily, as the verse cited above is showing that slavery is not something one should take in lightly on themselves.

If freedom has been lost, then, personally, make sure it is protected at the societal level by instituting state laws about it, which allowed the mistake or misfortune of becoming slaves to be corrected.

Don't be harsh with slaves (human dignity is important).

Humans are truly recognising their value before God if they are in His will.

In the New Testament, the slaves in the Roman Empire were encouraged to become free if they can (1 Corinthians 7:21), but otherwise, be respectful to their master.
In Christ, there is no slave of free but Christ is all and in all (Galatians 3:28). Some former slaves even became pope[36].

---

[36] Fr. Paolo O. Pirlo, SHMI (1997). "St. Callistus I". *My First Book of Saints*. Sons of Holy Mary Immaculate - Quality Catholic Publications. p. 240

(32) HOMOSEXUALITY

Christianity is scripturally locked into the concept that God views homosexuality as an abomination. There are many verses in both the Old and New Testament confirming this point. If the churches accept homosexuality as an authentic alternative lifestyle, it would be an admission that the scriptures are wrong. However, to hold steady on this issue will further alienate the growing tide of people, most notably the young, who view it as a matter of equality. Christianity loses no matter which direction it goes. And the Bible and Judeo-Christianity lose credibility for not having foresight on this issue.

RESPONSE

There are 6 verses in the Bible that discusses homosexuality directly and many indirectly, like "God created them male and female" (Genesis 5:2; Matthew 19:4), which confirms that it is a sin before God. The true Christians tend not to ask themselves, "How would society perceive me/us?" and then base the answer on their conviction, but a true Christian asks the question, "What does God want and what is best for the individual?" because both parts of the question complement each other.
Those people of this world who support gay marriage are mostly concerned with matters of equality which is good motivation, but they elevate the point of view of the person and their desires above what is generally good for them before God. Christians, on the other hand, are expected to be concerned foremostly with the good will of God on earth for everyone and the prospect of eternal life for each individual.

Equality, therefore, is important, but living a life closer to God, spiritually enjoyable, avoiding eternal punishment, and being in God's joyful and loving presence forever is more important.

The faithful Christian church would remain steady in its position to love and not do evil to the sinner, but at the same time, warn them that the sin they do, when fully developed, causes death.

God wouldn't change His position because He loves us and His character of loving Father is unchanged. He would keep on calling us, for our wellbeing, to repent from every sin which includes homosexual lifestyle.

(33) STATUS OF WOMEN

There are numerous scriptures in the Bible that clearly pronounce that a man is superior to a woman, which was consistent with the times it was written. Consider the following scriptures:

1 Corinthians 11:3:

But I want you to realize that the head of every man is Christ, and the head of the woman is man, and the head of Christ is God.

1 Corinthians 11:8-9:

For man did not come from woman, but woman from man; neither was man created for woman, but woman for man.

But times have changed. Societies the world over have bent over backwards to give women equal status and opportunity. Most marriages are now viewed as a 50/50 venture, a two-person team, as opposed to a master and a helper. The sticking point is that a real God and those he allegedly inspired would have foreseen this ultimate evolution of societal mores.

RESPONSE

The Bible offers a unique view of the relationship between a husband and wife. On one hand, she should respect him deeply and realise that spiritually, he has authority over her, and on another, they are equal partners before God ("there is no male or female" (Galatians 3:28)).

The husband is expected to be her spiritual "master," not in a way of dominating her as if she is his slave but lovingly care for her and make her feel happy. He has to aim to take care of her needs as Christ does for the Church's.

Sarah was calling Abraham "master" and yet, at some point, she practically ordered him to send away his son and his other wife (a servant in the house), and even though he was reluctant, God told him, "Listen to the voice of your wife." (Genesis 21:12). Sarah was anything but a consonant in the family. There is no clash because it is about the attitude of the heart of deep respect to spiritual, family authority, and not slavish and abject obedience.

It's so important that the man should make his wife happy that in Israel, very interestingly, if people get together, the man should stay at least 1 year with his wife.

"If a man has recently married, he must not be sent to war or have any other duty laid on him. For one year he is to be free to stay at home and bring happiness to the wife he has married" (Deuteronomy 24:5).

Christ submits to the Father and the church to Christ (Ephesians 5:24), and this means unity and perfection. In a similar way, when the man submits to Christ and His word, it wouldn't be a great thing for the woman to submit to him because she is not a slave of his personal whims or preferences but a follower of the love and authority of God.

Christ is equal to the Father and He submits in everything to Him and the Father loves the Son and grants everything the Son wants. Similarly, the wife is equal to her husband but chooses to be submissive to him, and he loves her so much that he wants to grant everything she wishes in accordance with God's will.

These verses could certainly be abused as nearly everything in the Bible, but those people who can live it out as it is said in the Scripture would have a very happy and close relationship, and would be as a family very close to God.

(34) LACK OF SCIENTIFIC INSIGHT

The Bible lacks any insights related to science that were not understood at the time and includes many of the then-current scientific misunderstandings. The two creation myths in Genesis are good examples. What should be troubling to a Christian is why this is so. Wouldn't the maker of the universe have communicated some basic truths about the world, such as the germ theory of disease to alleviate a lot of needless suffering? The absence of new ideas about science in the Bible is evidence that it was written by men with no inspiration from a supernatural being.

RESPONSE

The Bible actually contains numerous scientific insights which were not prevalent until recent times. Let's look at a few of them which could not easily be, or at all, known through natural means at disposal to the people back then (over 3000 years ago).

One thing is that God created everything from nothing. God said and it happened, "Let there be light." (Genesis 1:3).
Just up until the early 2000s, many scientists still believed that the universe and especially time is eternal[37]. Now, it has been proven that it had a beginning. And the most plausible explanation, which can be inferred from material knowledge, is that it began from nothing but energy as there is nothing else

---

[37] http://www.hawking.org.uk/the-origin-of-the-universe.html

that fits the bill[38]. Furthermore, the sum of total energy, after deducting the dark energy from the material energy, in the universe is zero[39]. Scripture tells us that the universe is like "nothing" (Isaiah 40:15-17) before God. It exists only because God "said".

The Bible clearly tells us also that God is personal, "God is spirit" (John 4:24), which accounts for how from blind energy the creation can get to intelligible universe. But God was understood as power at the same time. Jesus said: "But I tell you, from now on you will see the Son of Man seated at the right hand of the Power and coming on the clouds of heaven" (Matthew 26:64).

Hence, we already have three things with enormous scientific consequences which the Bible tells us about the universe, two of which modern science agrees with and the other we hope it will get to a conclusion in due course - nothingness, energy, and intelligence as the first causes.

Agreeing with the first two was not easy to come by. We should know that even Albert Einstein was so wedded to this belief that the universe is eternal that he couldn't get around the idea of its finitude or time limit for many years. He devised the idea of "gravitational effect" to explain the findings showing beginning.[40][41]

Also, we are told in the Bible that God holds everything together against the law of entropy (the tendency of everything to deteriorate into simple particles) through His Word and intelligence (Colossians 1:17, Hebrews 1:3). The "power" or "force" which is not material is the source of everything material and the divine intellect which is expressed through God's powerful Word is holding everything together into existence. Interestingly, today, the field of physics sees the field of force as

---

[38] http://www.bbc.co.uk/earth/story/20141106-why-does-anything-exist-at-all
[39] https://www.astrosociety.org/publication/a-universe-from-nothing/
[40] https://www.nationalgeographic.com/magazine/2005/05/einstein-relativity-cosmology-space-time-big-bang/
[41] https://www.space.com/9593-einstein-biggest-blunder-turns.html

most fundamental to existence and not material substance (http://www.thenewatlantis.com/publications/the-genius-and-faith-of-faraday-and-maxwell).

Another example, now on a very practical level, is the biblical instruction to cover and do away with excrements and wash things with running water. In Deuteronomy 23:12,13, God told the Israelites to relieve themselves outside the camp, which we could understand in general as nobody likes the human odours, but He also tells them to COVER it well with earth under the pain of punishment. Up until the beginning of the 20th Century, there were many people and especially those who were camping for a long time like in a war campaign, who died because of poor handling of excrements and low hygiene.
Then, further example, in Leviticus 15:13, the Israelites are told to wash themselves and clothes, which were possibly contaminated, in running water (Leviticus 15:13) - not standing, but running water. You cannot see with the naked eye the difference between washing something in a big pot of water and washing in the river, but when there is a possibility for spreading of germs, the instruction is "wash in running water."

Many eminent scientists through history insisted that the revelations of the Bible inspired them in their research. Matthew Fontaine Maury was clear that the Bible for him is an important inspiration and his main discovery in the science of oceanography, "the paths of the sea," was triggered by the verse "the birds of the heavens, and the fish of the sea, whatever passes along the paths of the seas" (Psalm 8:8). He was clear that "the Bible is authority for everything it touches."[42]

Michael Faraday, who has got a dozen or more laws, observations, phenomena and discoveries bearing his name like the Faraday cage, the Faraday constant, Faraday's law of

---
[42] Lewis, 1927, p. 99

induction, the Faraday (rotation) effect, the farad (a unit of electrical capacitance), and so on, once said, "God has been pleased to work on his material creation by laws... the Creator governs his material works by definite laws resulting from the forces impressed on matter." (ibid)

The historian Geoffrey Cantor, in his 1991 biography of Faraday, argues that Faraday's understanding of the consistency and simplicity of nature was not only the result of his scientific work but also a premise of it; it was intrinsic to the metaphysical presuppositions that directed his research. He sought the unifying laws relating the forces of the world and was highly successful in finding these laws for electricity, magnetism, and light. Faraday's metaphysical principles sometimes functioned as necessary truths and other times as guiding principles." (Ibid)

God tells Adam and Eve in Genesis 1:28 that they should "fill" the earth and "submit" it. He has given humanity the ability to figure out how nature works and the logic behind it shows the genius of the greatest mind ever, the personal Creator, Spirit and One God.

(35) SPLINTERING

The surest sign of a man-made enterprise is that it splits quickly into many different factions. On the other hand, one initiated by a God would be expected to converge into a tight unity. This is because only those groups that aligned correctly with the divine theological blueprint would receive supernatural support and thereby flourish, attract members, and survive the long term. Any wayward factions would lose favor and couldn't compete for new members.

There are now more than 41,000 Christian denominations, many of which have very disparate beliefs and practices. This is a valid clue that Christianity is a man-made concept.

RESPONSE

Division may seem like an entirely bad thing but this is not what the Bible says because the reality is more nuanced. Apostle Paul insists that, "There must be factions among you in order that those who are genuine among you may be recognized." (1 Corinthians 11:19).

Very often, in some churches, you find people who want to sincerely serve God and some who are there for other motives. When those who care for the purity of the faith and what the Bible says clash with those who prefer to please men, government, or seek their own interests, then there might be a time for a split.

It is true that the denominations who distance themselves from the Bible tend to be anaemic and gradually diminish or haemorrhage members to other more Bible-based traditional values espousing churches. We have seen this historically happen through the splits early on with heresies like the Adoptionists, Docetists, Ebionites, Arians, etc. and later through the Reformation, Anabaptists, and nowadays the Charismatic and Pentecostal movement, and partly also some resurgence of reformed Christianity. Yet it is never clear cut. The supernatural follows those who have faith and who follow the Word of Jesus but in every denomination, we may see someone who was once led powerfully by God and then gradually declined in faith and fell in terrible sin and sometimes even off the faith.

Apostle Paul says: "The Lord knows those who are his," and, "Everyone who confesses the name of the Lord must turn away from iniquity." (2 Timothy 2:19).

In the end, only God knows who His true people are. Still, there is one sign common to all of them - they have turned away from iniquity. We should note that mostly the vast majority of the Christian denominations agree on the basic Nicene creed of faith[43] and often the divisions are over important in their basic meaning, but not putting at stake the salvation of the soul matters.

For example, the Baptists insist on water baptism by immersion, accept that people can be baptised in the Holy Spirit and have the sign speaking in tongues, but do not agree with child baptism as Anglicans do and neither readily preach and insist that their members should actively seek the experience of baptism in the Holy Spirit with tongues. Hence, in a traditional Baptist church, you have many faithful Christians who were once baptised as children and such people who speak in tongues when they pray, although the majority are not.

In the Pentecostal churches, full immersion baptism in water is the norm but unlike the Baptists, "the Baptism of fire" is expected of all believers and they are encouraged to seek God for it and the sign of unknown tongues. In a good Pentecostal

---

[43] http://anglicansonline.org/basics/nicene.html

church, most people report that they have this experience and ability. Some Charismatics, unlike the traditional Pentecostals, say that speaking in tongues is only one of the signs alongside other supernatural manifestations of the spirit of God. Some Reformed churches would say that there are no supernatural gifts at work anymore but God had given the miracles and gifts of the Spirit to the early church in order to establish the reality of the Gospel in the world, and now, with that done, the gifts have ceased.

The Catholics would insist on the special place of Mary the mother of Jesus and, of course, the Pope and his infallible word when said ex cathedra (from the pulpit). Generally, the protestants would reject these Catholic notions. The Catholics, though, unlike many of the Reformed Protestant Christians, would accept the supernatural gifts and they also have a huge charismatic renewal amongst them going on.

Every one of these denominations would agree on the basics of the faith: there is One God in three eternal persons - Father, Son and Holy Spirit. The Person of Jesus the Son) became a man, died on the cross for the sins of the world and was resurrected on the third day in confirmation that He is indeed the Son of God. He is interceding for all Christians who call on His Name and is coming back in glory to take His church with Him. Everybody who believes in Him and trusts in Him in obedience would be saved. Although there are differences they do agree on. Hence, the power of God in God-given measure is with them because God confirms His truth.

Some people prefer more liturgical church, like with the Catholicism, and only organ playing inside, others prefer the good old hymns of Wesley brothers, and some prefer the modern pop songs of Hillsong Church. The hand has five digits (fingers and thumb), which are different in some ways but they all serve and function toward one goal of benefiting the whole body. So the church may differ in its denominations, but it's members serve each other and the world, and seek to reflect the love of Jesus.

(36) THE WAY THINGS HAPPEN

The events in the world proceed with no evidence of manipulation by gods, devils, demons, angels, or anything else of the like. We see natural disasters, plagues, wars, mass shootings, and all sorts of mayhem without any evidence that these tragedies are being controlled or planned for any purpose whatsoever.

An existence overseen by supernatural forces would look very different. There would be a detectable sense of an outside influence and violations of scientific principles such as gravity, entropy, or the conservation of mass and energy. Instead we see none of these effects, just a world fully consistent with the absence of a God.

RESPONSE

Miracles are defined either as unlikely events defying the laws of nature or such events which are extremely rare but within the boundaries of the natural laws.
God has created a world which is working as an intricate system. It is odd to think that there should be miracles of the first kind happening all the time and at all levels. This would mean chaos and lack of any predictability. Our intellect would be superfluous because logical inference wouldn't work. But God is not a God of chaos (1 Corinthians 14:33). This means that when God does miracles of the first kind, they wouldn't disrupt and alter the world unless it is a punishment. Punishment is chaos magnified and control over the situation lost, but even then it looks that God does it within the boundaries of the natural laws.

A few examples.

God made the Red Sea part before the Israelites but this is not something Moses could do always and at will. If he could, then why build ships at all? Why learn to navigate the sea? How would the human intellect develop if he would do everything exclusively supernaturally? But this miracle could have also been a very natural "miracle" like the hurricane Irma, which demonstrated how it is quite possible for hurricane to happen if there is a strong wind by sucking up big swaths of the ocean. So this is an example of a miracle within the framework of the natural laws.

The miracle with multiplying the bread and fish which Jesus did is more likely one of the first kind - it defies the natural laws as we know them. Why would Jesus not do this all the time, even though He had supporters like Maria, Johanna and Susan (Luke 8:1-3) who were "helping them out from their property"? Because the miracles are part of the Christian life, but not the majority of it. They happen here and there and this boosts our faith and we want to seek God even more, but most of the time, we live in the natural world and have to follow the natural laws of how the world operates.

Therefore, the existence of supernatural being does not mean chaos and detectable constant influence over nature, but actually, it means order and harmony, whilst on a subtle level, God is holding and sustaining all things.

 Surely, the world is not ideal and God says that it is not because it has been touched by evil, and that's why God promised to renew it at the end of time. God is the only guarantor that the oasis of order and friendliness to life and human life in particular would continue to exist here on earth. There is no reason to think that the very existence of life on earth as we experience it, given the utter unwelcoming state of the known universe, is not a miracle in itself.

So the existence of the green planet Earth in its harmony and order, conducive to life, is a strong clue of the existence of the eternal Designer, Protector, and Holder behind it.

At the same time, the miracles, most of the time, are orderly circumstances which benefit those who seek God, and very occasionally, they happen without ready explanation of how they do but are real nonetheless.

God's mind is unfathomable.

(37) FICTIONAL STORIES

Many people believe the Bible is the inerrant word of God, but, for that to be true, it must stand up to critical analysis as a factual history. Any deviation from this ideal would mean that any other portions of the Bible, even the otherwise believable stories, would be suspect for their veracity. Most Biblical stories cannot be proven true or false, but, as an example, the following ten can be considered false beyond a reasonable doubt:

Garden of Eden: Modern science has long surpassed this amateurish explanation of our origins

The Great Flood: There is no evidence of a worldwide flood

Census in the gospels: The Romans took great care in documenting their censuses; there was no census at the time of Jesus' birth, and there was never a requirement for people to travel to their birth cities to be counted

Passover prisoner release: The Romans never released a prisoner at the Passover

He who is without sin: The story of Jesus and the woman caught in adultery was added to the scriptures almost 400 years after the fact and was copied from a previous religious tradition

Hebrew enslavement in Egypt: Absolutely no evidence from any source including Egyptian historical records exist for this

Camel archaeology: Camels were discussed in the Old Testament before any camels existed there

Zombies after Jesus death: Matthew's account of people rising from their graves, walking around the city, and conversing with people is false based on its intrinsic absurdity

Elisha calling down a curse of boys who were mocking him resulting in two bears emerging from the woods and mauling 42 children: False by reason of absurdity

The Tower of Babel: Linguistic studies reveal this explanation for different languages to be farcical

These are just some of many examples, but they are sufficient to show that the Bible contains a lot of fiction and the extent to which it pervades the book is unknown. It calls into question every story presented in the Bible as being potentially fictional or otherwise exaggerated.

RESPONSE

The Bible is indeed inerrant about everything which it states to be the case and which has important connotation regarding its message of salvation and knowing who God is. Its basic message which concerns the truth is absolutely true. There may be some small details which do not affect its message and which could not be precisely related or told, but this, if this is the case, should be proven objectively.

As it stands, there are very few things said in it and always minutia ones (which may mean semantical problem not an issue with factology) that could be seriously questioned. We should remember that it is a divinely inspired book written by over 40 humans. It would be surprising if there is no "mistake" in it because humans by definition do make mistakes, even when doing the will of God, sometimes. But it assures us that it is generally and specifically regarding the salvation of man and who God truly is, and there is nothing in it which misleads the person regarding what God has done for them and what His will is.

Let's examine the examples given and see if they are really "errors".

Garden of Eden
This was a place where the earliest humans lived in safety far from the threats of the rest of the fallen world which was touched by the power of evil. Why is it hard to believe that there was a time when the first humans found themselves in a place which was protected and good for them in order to help them thrive? Humans had to find some kind of environmental equilibrium and the result is that they managed to pass on their genes successfully.

What kind of trace do we want to find of it today when the Bible clearly says that humans were expelled from this place and it was inaccessible any longer? There are great cities like Memphis and indeed civilisations which have left next to nothing today. Eden goes much further back than that to the primordial time.

Hence, the rejection of its existence lies on the wrong assumptions.

The Great Flood
The Bible tells us about flood which killed all living mammals (animals breathing in through their nostrils) on earth. We are not sure whether when it says "all the earth under heaven was covered in water" it means literally all of it, or it means all the

earth where there were mammals and was accessible to them. What is important here is that the entirety of mammal life, and particularly humans, except some God-providence exceptions on the planet, was destroyed, as this was the only way it could be saved from complete self-destruction.

Some scientists see the manifold layers of strata all over the world as a sign of the worldwide flood, others think that this was not only one event but many such occurrences on a smaller scale over a long period of time[44].

We know that life on earth was under threat due to natural cataclysms and this is borne out by science. The Bible explains this as a disaster caused by "perversion," "violence," immorality and entertaining and "imagining only evil." And this cause of the disaster described in Genesis is absolutely true and there is no way to be proven otherwise, as we can see, even today, how easily natural resources could be squandered, and piling up weapons could mean another destruction of the world as we know it. All that is uncontrollably tragic for the whole humanity is due to lack of moral fibre in all the people on earth.

The warning which the Bible gives through this story is very timely and relevant. Did the flood happen? We have no reason to think that the flood that annihilated all living mammals and birds never occurred, although it's globality is disputed.

The phrase "kol erezt" appears about 200 times in the Bible and in only less than a quarter of them does it means "all the earth per se." This means that the flood could have not been global, but enormous enough to upend all mammal and bird life everywhere.

Census in the gospels

As we discussed in chapter 20, Luke was "a first class historian" and what he meant to tell us was true, even though there may be

---

[44] https://web.stanford.edu/~meehan/donnellyr/summary.html

some confusion around this again as often happens due to false assumptions.

Passover prisoner release
The Bible clearly states that Pilate had "the custom" to let a prisoner go free. Knowing that he had trouble governing the province, this is not an unlikely attempt to placate his subjects.

Story adulterae
We touched on this story in chapter 17 and we can see that it has been quoted much earlier by the early church fathers, and its absence in the best manuscripts has most likely to do with how the Lectionary was managed, its relegation to the end of John, and, hence, loss. There is space for it though in the text left in one of the best manuscripts we have available. The flow of the story in John without it is not that good. Crucially, it doesn't contradict the Scripture and the character of Jesus and God as revealed in the rest of the Bible. Based on this, we can be confident in its truthfulness.

Hebrew enslavement in Egypt
There are records of Semitic people coming down into Egypt to purchase food and some to stay in the country. There are records of famines. At some point, apparently Semitic people (non Israeli) were practically having a kingdom in Northern Egypt. In Egypt, there were many Semites over extended periods of times. Some were free, others were slaves.

The Biblical account tells us that the Israelites left Egypt in a very traumatic way for the Egyptians due to the stubbornness of their leader, Pharaoh. Then this event is unlikely to make it into their records because their way of writing history was highly selective. For example, they never lost a battle. They may win one after another and next, they were closer to home (indicating retreat), but officially, they always won. The circumstantial evidence suggests that it is absolutely possible that the Israelites were there and the Bible is right about this as with so many other things.

Camel archaeology

Bactrian camels were domesticated sometime around 2500 BC or earlier in Asia. Dromedarian camels' first place of domestication was probably the Arabian peninsula around the same time.
In any case, in Israel, the camels were already widely used by 930 BC.
Abraham lived in Canaan around 2000-1800 BC. We should realise that he was a very rich man and although others could not afford camels, he could. The number of these animals in the region, though, was so small that it did not leave any significant record. He might have had 20 or 30 of them. The evidence is hard to be found buried in the earth given that much latter on, in the beginning of the first millennium, there were possibly tens of thousands of them in Israel and yet the excavated remains are maybe less than a hundred.
Most organic matter dissolves and only a small fraction of it remains in the ground to be found by the archaeologists. The smaller amount of initial matter, the less would be found in modern times.

Resurrected saints

The Gospel of Matthew (27:50) tells us that after Jesus' resurrection, "many bodies of dead saints were resurrected." Of course, in a materialistic framework, any supernatural event like the resurrection is dismissed as impossible. But that's the point of the Gospel - to show us that God is real and He conquered the law of death and weakness. For those people who had a supernatural encounter, this is very real and possible. If Jesus resurrected from the dead, it is absolutely believable that other people did as well. He is the "first fruit" leading the way to all others.

Elisha and the boys torn up by the bears
In 2 Kings 2:23, prophet Elisha was harassed by some boys. Then he cursed them in the name of God and two bears appeared a bit later and killed 42 of them. As a prophet, he could see if these boys were not going to change their ways but will surely become even worse and cause a lot of suffering to other people. When God allows such curse to work, this means there is no way of repentance possible. God is longsuffering and patient (Exodus 34:6). If there was a slight chance they would change their ways, then we think they would have been spared.

The Tower of Babel

The linguists agree that there are proto-languages, from which modern tongues evolved. What the story of Babel tells us regarding the languages is that there is one most basic proto-language for all and that the evolution of all subsequent ones happened alongside the separation between the groups (which was the point of God). Languages tend to evolve for a relatively short amount of time, maybe several hundred years, to the point of becoming foreign to the listener - compare medieval and modern English. We don't know how long the tower was built for but it could have been 100, 500 or more years. Maybe different groups of people were responsible for different things and materials and they got together based on specialisation and over time they drifted apart from the rest and after some time of isolation, the new language evolved.

This could be absolutely possible or it might have been a miracle, but the point that there was only one language once and that languages evolve and go their separate ways is generally accepted by all who study the subject. For unbelievers, this is due to natural causes, but for the Bible, God's finger on this occasion was in it regardless of the way He chose to do it.

What we see is that the author of these objections is looking to pass a judgment on the Biblical veracity based on his materialistic worldview,[45] but did not want to do his homework and look for any plausible, reasonable explanation of these stories.

---

[45] The belief that everything that exists is matter or a function of it

(38) THE TEN COMMANDMENTS

The Ten Commandments have been presented as the ultimate guide to human morality. But a close inspection reveals that only five have a meaningful impact: do not steal, do not perjure, do not kill, don't commit adultery, and honor your parents. Just as revealing is what is not included:

No proscription of slavery
No proscription of child endangerment
No proscription of bigotry
No proscription of racism
No proscription of sexism
No proscription of classism
No proscription of blackmail or bribery
No proscription of discrimination against LGBTQ persons
No proscription of incest
No proscription of torture or terrorism
No proscription of rape
No proscription against the mistreatment, exploitation, and relocation of native populations
No command to treat animals humanely
No command to take care of the Earth's environment
No command to help others in need
No command to settle disputes peacefully
No command to distribute the Earth's resources fairly

It should be obvious that an all-knowing, all-wise, all-discerning, supernatural God could have devised a much better set of rules for mankind, a set that would have placed humanity on a more peaceful, loving, and kind trajectory that the one we have experienced.

RESPONSE

The Ten Commandments are not the ultimate detailed guide on how one should behave but the foundational rules of life. They are summed up by the two most basic commandments "Love the Lord your God with all your heart, your soul, your mind and power" and "Love your neighbour as yourself."
Jesus says, "On these two commandments hang all the Law and the prophets" (Matthew 22:40).
If you love your neighbour as yourself, you would not do bad to anybody.
The Biblical moral code is based on those commandments - 2 plus 10.
Every other rule and prescription is influenced by their logic and direction.
Examples:

Slavery - "You were bought at a price. Do not become slaves of men" (1 Corinthians 7:23); "If any of your fellow Israelites become poor and sell themselves to you, do not make them work as slaves" (Leviticus 25:39).
No human being should be exploited and crushed by the inhumane conditions of work and existence.

Child endangerment - "If you then, though you are evil, know how to give good gifts to your children, how much more will your Father in heaven give good gifts to those who ask him!" (Matthew 7:11); "Children are heritage from the Lord, and the fruit of the womb is a reward" (Psalm 127:3).
Clearly, children had to be cared for and even evil people should find it normal to look after their children and protect them. They are regarded as a great blessing.

Bigotry - "Accept the one whose faith is weak, without quarreling over disputable matters" (Romans 14:1); "But if serving the LORD seems undesirable to you, then choose for yourselves this day whom you will serve, whether the gods your ancestors served beyond the Euphrates, or the gods of the Amorites, in whose land you are living. But as for me and my household, we will serve the LORD." (Joshua 24:15)

Certainly, there is a choice. One can choose what to believe and whom to serve. Yet, to use an analogy with the political parties, you cannot believe in nationalisation of the private sector and run as a Republican. It is not intolerant if people do not vote for you in the primaries due to your convictions.

The Bible lets you live the way you like but says that you cannot be part of God's people if you cross the boundaries of right and wrong before God; however, you have significant freedom within those boundaries for your good. Is that not the case with every organisation and country? There are always boundaries. Some a merely human and man-made but the Biblical value system is of God and for those who want to serve Him.

Racism - "The foreigner residing among you must be treated as your native-born. Love them as yourself, for you were foreigners in Egypt. I am the LORD your God" (Leviticus 19:34).

"You are to love those who are foreigners, for you yourselves were foreigners in Egypt" (Deuteronomy 10:19)

We can see how the foreigners were protected in spite of their race or ethnicity and they were equaled to anybody else from Israel.

Sexism - Jesus appeared to women first. He asked them to go and tell others about His resurrection, even though the cultural weight of woman's testimony was not equal with man's. Jesus showed that they are absolutely reliable and equal to men and they were the first evangelists. We see apostles amongst women too. In Romans 16:7, Apostle Paul says, "Greet Andronicus and

Junia, my countrymen and my fellow prisoners, who are of note among the apostles, who also were in Christ before me." He accepted Junia as apostle even before him!

There is nothing in the Bible to suggest that the women have less rights before God and their work or opinions are of less value than men's. Yes, the culture of the ancient people was such that women were counted as second hand people, but this is not how God made it to be and how He envisaged it.

Classism - "Learn to do right. See that justice is done — help those who are oppressed, give orphans their rights, and defend widows" (Isaiah 1:17); "Don't take advantage of the poor just because you can; don't take advantage of those who stand helpless in court. The Lord will argue their case for them and threaten the life of anyone who threatens theirs" (Proverbs 22:22-23).

We see that those who belong to lower social status at the moment and are weaker are defended by God. There is a severe warning for those who trample their rights.

Blackmail - This is included in the commandment, "Do not covet anything belonging to your neighbour" (Exodus 20:17).

Bribery - "The greedy bring ruin to their households, but the one who hates bribes will live" (Proverbs 15:27); "Do not accept a bribe, for a bribe blinds those who see and twists the words of the innocent" (Exodus 23:8)

The Bible is quite firm and serious about bribes and how they affect justice. Justice and righteousness alongside knowing God are the key ideas behind the commandments of God.

Discrimination against LGBTQ persons

The homosexual lifestyle is indeed condemned in the Bible, but it is not singled out from other forms of sin or sexual sin. It is on a par with any sex outside the heterosexual relationship of marriage. We do not need to repeat the verses which treat this issue, but clearly, like with every sin, God wants to forgive, purify, and restore in Christ.

Incest - "If a man marries his sister, the daughter of either his father or his mother, and they have sexual relations, it is a disgrace. They are to be publicly removed from their people. He has dishonored his sister and will be held responsible" (Leviticus 20:17).
Incest is widely discussed in Leviticus 18:8-18, 20:11-21. It is something which Moses was ordered to make custom in Israel to avoid in spite of previous experience with it by people like Abraham, Lot, and others.

Torture or terrorism - "Do not kill" (Exodus 20:13) and "Do not harm or want anything which belongs to your neighbour" (Exodus 20:17) certainly prohibit that. "Love does no harm to a neighbour. Therefore, love is the fulfilment of the law" (Romans 13:10). No comment is necessary, as these verses point out what we need to know regarding the issue of torture and terrorism.

Rape - 25 "But if in the open country a man meets a young woman who is betrothed, and the man seizes her and lies with her, then only the man who lay with her shall die. 26 "But you shall do nothing to the young woman; she has committed no offense punishable by death. For this case is like that of a man attacking and murdering his neighbour" - Deuteronomy 22:25-26
We see that the Bible is quite serious about rape. It's equaled in some ways to murder and is given the death penalty. Some confuse verses which talk about a man sleeping with a virgin woman without being married to her as if the rape is tolerated. In fact, if the woman is betrothed this still carries the death penalty and if she is not, he should take care of her and not leave her, which she would normally expect. If she wants not to be with him, she can opt out but this was not the culture back then.

Women's greatest achievement in life was to get married and have children.

The mistreatment, exploitation, and relocation of native populations
This is again covered by the "Love your neighbour as yourself" command.
In the Bible, there is indeed a case when seven tribes were expelled from the land of Canaan but only when the level of their bad behaviour reaches its apex. God gave them hundreds of years to clean their act. He told Abraham about his children: "And they shall come back here in the fourth generation, for the iniquity of the Amorites is not yet complete." (Genesis 15:16).
So the Israelites were only able to take over this land because the social practices of that population have become inhumane. They were guilty of tolerating, approving and glorifying incest, bestiality, homosexual practices and rape, child sacrifice, social injustice and violence and many other sins: "For the people of the land, who were before you, did all of these abominations, so that the land became unclean" (Leviticus 18:27). This made for a really sad profile of that society, which was only going worse. God is fair, though. At some point, Israel has to leave the land into captivity because they lost a tragic war, which loss was attributed to their embedded sinful practices over a long period of time with no chance of correction.
About the nations which were not in a state of such depravity, God said:
"Do not contend with them, for I will not give you any of their land, no, not so much as for the sole of the foot to tread on." - Deuteronomy 2:5

- Not treating animals humanely

From the beginning of creation, God prescribed vegetarian diet: "And God said, 'Behold, I have given you every plant yielding seed that is on the face of all the earth, and every tree with seed in its fruit. You shall have them for food.'" - Genesis 1:29

This was changed later on - maybe in order to respond to the growing needs of sustenance of the population - but the prophets sometime talk about the later days when all people and animals would be vegetarians again: "The cow and the bear shall graze; their young shall lie down together; and the lion shall eat straw like the ox" (Isaiah 11:7), "They shall not hurt or destroy in all my holy mountain; for the earth shall be full of the knowledge of the LORD as the waters cover the sea" (Isaiah 11:9). God's ideal world is one without any violence and cruelty. The more the character of God is known, the more the world will change.

There is one story which shows how the angel of God seriously rebukes a prophet for hitting his donkey: 32 And the angel of the LORD said to him, "Why have you struck your donkey these three times? Behold, I have come out to oppose you because your way is perverse before me. 33 The donkey saw me and turned aside before me these three times. If she had not turned aside from me, surely just now I would have killed you and let her live." - Numbers 22:32-33

We can see how displeased God is to see the donkey being treated in an inhumane manner and how his punishment would have been very discriminate, omitting the animal but inflicting displeasure on the greedy and cruelly behaving man.

Not taking care of the Earth's environment

The first command that God gave Adam was not a prohibition but a positive one: "The LORD God took the man and put him in the Garden of Eden to work it and keep it." - Genesis 2:15.

God placed Adam in a garden which he had to work and keep. "Work" means putting an effort into maintaining the beautiful environment and making the best out of it. "Keep" means to protect it and ensure that the resources of the earth are not merely used but acquired intelligently with great care for its substance and endurance.

The Israelites had to maintain hygiene and cleanliness all over where they were. They wouldn't camp and then just leave a lot of human waste. They would even be instructed to bury their excremental waste.

"And you shall have a trowel with your tools, and when you sit down outside, you shall dig a hole with it and turn back and cover up your excrement." - Deuteronomy 23:13.

God insisted that the whole camp must be clean and well maintained. How much they cared for the environment was a condition for their success: "Because the LORD your God walks in the midst of your camp, to deliver you and to give up your enemies before you, therefore your camp must be holy, so that he may not see anything indecent among you and turn away from you." - Deuteronomy 23:14

It would be hard to imagine foul rivers, chemical-killed fish, and poisoned soil when this attitude of care for the natural environment is exercised.

Not helping others in need

Jesus clearly said that "it is better to give than to receive." (Acts 20:35).

Many of the commandments are directed to protect the neighbour as a very minimum, but they create a solid base, as with other ideas of how to live, to realise the precious nature of your neighbour and from then to do him good.

The Israelites even have orders to do good to their enemies!

4 "If you meet your enemy's ox or his donkey going astray, you shall bring it back to him. 5 If you see the donkey of one who hates you lying down under its burden, you shall refrain from leaving him with it; you shall rescue it with him." - Exodus 23:4-5

Not attempting to settle disputes peacefully

We should be honest, if you do not even think to attack and kill anybody or steal from them or lie against them or even want anything which belongs them, how would you ever be motivated to be violent when disputing? If you are actively urged to care for your neighbours as yourself, why would you seek a non-peaceful resolution? It does not make sense.

Not distributing the Earth's resources fairly.
This is a bit controversial for some, but the Israelites, in some way, were the most socially aware and equality seeking people before the church appeared. At some point, they were collecting manna from heaven and then were told to see how much each gathered and share it among themselves in such a way that they had enough for their needs.
"But when they measured it with an Omer, whoever gathered much had nothing left over, and whoever gathered little had no lack. Each of them gathered as much as he could eat." - Exodus 16:18

Actually, the Bible tells us that God provides everything necessary for human beings to thrive by doing what is good before Him.
"His divine power has granted to us all things that pertain to life and godliness, through the knowledge of him who called us to his own glory and excellence." - 2 Peter 1:3
As the verse says, though, the resources would be distributed rightly and everybody's needs would be supplied if people know God and realise what his plan of "glory and excellence" is for them.

We can see that the Bible provides answers to all moral concerns people may have, but it is not a rule-book. It is dynamic text which ensures one doesn't get stuck and rigid with merely cultural customs. It is very steady to the principle, too, meaning that the reader does not have to easily embrace and follow the next fashion of what is good and bad, which may change in accordance with the cultural trends. The Bible presents the eternal counsel of God, who always has what to say to people of every background, belief system, and time of existence, and He invites them to share with Him His truly loving and just nature.

(39) BORROWED MIRACULOUS ELEMENTS

Most of the miracles discussed in the Bible were common elements of pre-Christian pagan religions including:

Miraculous foretelling of a deity
Virgin birth
A guiding star
A nativity visit by royalty
The baby God threatened by a jealous ruler
Manifesting extraordinary wisdom in childhood
Turning water into wine
Walking on water
Enabling the lame to walk
Healing the sick
Raising up dead persons
Restoring sight to the blind
Allaying storms on the sea
Casting out devils
Communion with a holy meal representing the God's body
Being put to death
The sun becoming dark after the death
Rising from the dead
Talking to the disciples after resurrecting
Ascension into heaven
Providing salvation for mankind

The truth is that very few of the miracles discussed in the Bible are unique to Christianity. This is a strong piece of evidence that Christianity is a man-made,

cobbled, and fundamentally plagiarized faith.

RESPONSE

It is somewhat wrong to think that everything God does should be unique as an idea for His preferred group of people. People have strived to receive healing through nature or deities but this doesn't mean that God in Jesus "plagiarised" the practice. What is unique of Jesus is that nobody could do the level of miracles (quantity and greatness of them) as He did.
Let's look at each feature of His ministry mentioned and show its uniqueness.

Miraculous foretelling of a deity

Of course, many people would claim they know the future but uniquely for Jesus is that everything He said came to pass against great odds.

The Fall of Jerusalem and the establishment of the church are two unique prophecies which were unlikely to happen so soon and so spectacularly.
Judea was a well established province of the Roman Empire and they were even exempted from certain pagan cultic practices which were mandatory for others. Their religion was revered as one of the most ancient faiths and therefore it was tolerated a great deal. There were some unsuccessful revolts in the past like the one of Judas the Galilean (6AD), which showed that the Romans cannot and should not be challenged without serious repercussions.
When Jesus was preaching, there was a time of unknown, so far peace and prosperity for Judea. Yet Jerusalem fell in 70AD exactly as Jesus said. Moreover, Jerusalem was restored as a Jewish city as Jesus also said.

"They will fall by the edge of the sword and be led captive among all nations, and Jerusalem will be trampled underfoot by the Gentiles, until the times of the Gentiles are fulfilled." - Luke 21:24

Then, there is the advent of the church. Jesus said to faltering Peter:

"And I tell you, you are Peter, and on this rock I will build my church, and the gates of hell shall not prevail against it." - Matthew 16:18

How come that one cowardly, uneducated fisherman would lead 11 others more or less like him, in their lack of formal education and training, to establish the largest institution in the whole world - the Christian Church? From despised minority, the church grew into the most important factor in the society in 300 years, peacefully and without any bloodshed or violence, but then it was taken unfairly by its martyrs. Never before or after a peaceful group of people, which is at odds with its surrounding culture to the point of provoking disdain and persecution on many occasions, would have such a profound and lasting effect on the world around it, even till this very day. Jesus really knew what He was talking about. His words always come to pass.

Virgin birth

There is no identical birth recorded about anyone in history prior to Jesus. The three names which most often are mentioned are Horus, Dionysus, and Krishna. Horus was born after his mother helped resurrect her husband Osiris and fashioned a phallus out of gold for him.

Dionysus was also conceived through sexual intercourse between Zeus and a mortal woman called Samele. Krishna also had a mother, Devaki, and a father, Vasudeva. This is nothing like the virgin birth described by Matthew and Luke.

A guiding star

From ancient times, people have been following the guidance of the stars and particularly the Pole Star of the constellation, Ursa Minor, because it seems always steady and, therefore, is a good navigating signpost.

In the gospels, the wise men followed a peculiarly bright celestial body which they prophetically knew is leading them to where Jesus was. It may be that existing star was shining brighter or it was a new bright celestial body appearing, but the bottom line is that this cannot be really "plagiarised" and made a great deal of because following the stars was a common practice, not a great deal to be made of, and only Matthew mentioned it.

Surely, it wasn't so important for the other evangelists to include it in their accounts, although it has its own important significance.

A nativity visit by royalty

Jesus was visited by three wise men (not clarified if they were kings) but also by mere shepherds. Actually, the wise men found out through the stars about His birth, and the shepherds were told about it by angels. This is interesting because the Magi had to work hard to be able to recognise the stars in order to discern the new one in the sky, and they had to get an explanation by the scribes in Jerusalem where Christ would be born and then find Him, but the shepherds were immediately told where the Infant is. It seems God made it easier for the people of low social status to get to His Son.

The baby God threatened by a jealous ruler

Sadly, this was quite ordinary during those times. Any threat to the throne had to be eliminated. Solomon was willing to put his half-brother, Amnon, to death only because he wanted to have Abisag, who was sleeping with the elderly king David (without any intercourse as the Scripture explicitly points out), as his wife because they hoped she would help with his health (1 Kings 2:13-25).

In 2 Kings 11, queen Athaliah aimed to kill all the potential contenders for the throne of Judah, be they children or adults.

Vying for power, alas could lead to the annihilation of relatives or further off people who may be considered as a threat to the throne. Herod (d 4BC) was famous for his paranoid tendencies and he even killed members of his family, like his son, for being afraid they were clouding against him. So every potential new ruler who is perceived as a threat to the existing authorities could be in danger of persecution and death.

Manifesting extraordinary wisdom in childhood

Jesus is never presented in the gospels as one who had supernatural abilities as a child. By no means, He is said to have the wisdom and knowledge which He displayed later on. He was asking questions, though, and this impressed the rabbis. Certainly, He knew a lot but He was seemingly learning from them too. He was aware that He is the Son of God but He was learning things until it was time to reveal Himself to Israel. Luke says, "And Jesus increased in wisdom and in stature and in favor with God and man." (Luke 2:52).

This is a very different picture than the one drawn by the quasi-gospels like the Infant Gospel of Thomas, where you can see the made up streak clearly:

"When this boy, Jesus, was five years old, he was playing at the ford of a brook, and he gathered together into pools the water that flowed by, and made it at once clean, and commanded it by his word alone. But the son of Annas the scribe was standing there with Joseph, and he took a branch of a willow and (with it) dispersed the water which Jesus had gathered together. When Jesus saw what he had done, he was enraged and said to him:

'You insolent, godless dunderhead. What harm did the pools and the water do to you? See, now you also shall wither like a tree and shall bear neither leaves nor root nor fruits.' And immediately, that lad withered up completely."

The myth making was having certain black and white quality, which makes them recognisable to a modern reader but the gospels faithfully present the facts around Jesus and we see how His human and divine nature intertwine in a unique way. This way is not readily thought of if one sets out to create a myth.

Turning water into wine

There is no turning water into wine case recorded that occurred prior to Jesus. Moses and the Egyptians turned water into blood but not into wine. (Mithra) For Jesus to turn it into wine, this might have meant an almost total departure from the orthodox Jewish expectation of a miracle from God, given that wine is something people can abuse. But the connection between blood and wine becomes apparent in the Lord's Supper where the wine symbolises the blood of Jesus, which removes the sin, and which brings joy untold to the receiver (1 Peter 1:8).

Walking on water

Again, this is not something that special people or deities readily do, nor is it something we can read about in any human records prior to Jesus. There is one occasion described by a Buddhist writer (Buddhaghosa) but this is from around 5 century BC and, therefore, cannot be plagiarised.

Enabling the lame to walk

There is nobody who was recorded to have done this miracle in the way Jesus and His apostles did. It is very hard to find anyone prior to Christ performing this kind of miracles, let alone with such a great effect and detailed accounts from eyewitnesses. Jesus did it all the time, though.

Healing the sick

There are hundreds of "health and body wellness" deities in history but nobody is remotely like Jesus, who was amongst the people, responding to their requests, and often by saying a word only, and doing it with such an undeniable efficiency.

Raising up dead persons

This is extremely rare outside Judaism and Christianity. In the Bible, there are about 10 cases of resurrections of dead people. This makes it really peculiar to the Bible with some small exceptions, which we find elsewhere, that are not so much about real people as in the Bible, but concerns some kind of superheroes, like Oziris for example, who nobody knew if they were historical persons at all. Jesus is very much historically attested as a real person, who existed 2000 years ago.

Restoring sight to the blind

The man in his 40s', whose vision Jesus restored, said that there is no tradition in Israel for a blind person from birth to be given new sight. "Nobody has ever heard of opening the eyes of a man born blind" (John 9:32).
Elisha asked God to give sight to some Syrian soldiers (2 Kings 6:17), but this was a case of temporary blindness. It is again very hard to find anyone prior to Jesus (after Him it was His disciples doing it) who opened the eyes of the blind as a historical record.

Allaying storms on the sea

There are deities like Poseidon who may be able to stop the storm of the sea in Greek mythology, but they were never real people, or able to operate through people who are historically attested. Long before the myth about Poseidon, though, in the Psalms, God, Yahweh, is calming the sea.
"He stilled the storm to a whisper; the waves of the sea were hushed" (Psalm 107:29).
So, God was doing, through His Son, Jesus, being in the flesh, something He was already doing before anyway, and crucially, the accounts about it are before the Greek or other myths.

Casting out devils

This is a common practice since ancient times but Jesus was special in the way He was doing it.
"That evening they brought to him many who were oppressed by demons, and he cast out the spirits with a word and healed all who were sick." - Matthew 8:16

Josephus reports that Jewish exorcists were using root extracts and sacrifices to allay the suffering of the demon burdened. The Hindu practitioners were saying mantras, burning sacrificial fire and reciting some parts of their books in order to help. Often, practitioners do a kind of elaborate ritual procedures in order to help the victim of demonisation or for protection of people afraid of it.

Jesus was casting our fears and torments with one word. There was no demon too hard for Him to expel from the sufferer.

Communion with a holy meal representing God's body

It is impossible to find the exact resemblance of this sacrament in any other religion. Some people merely suggest that this may be the case with the cult of Dionysius for example, where it is thought, not clearly stated, that whilst drinking wine, the participants were part taking on the blood of the deity. In some legends, the wine is poured out as a libation, so there is not a clear cut practice as with the Christians, although many pagan attackers of Christianity went out of their way to even mock this special event. Drinking wine from one cup was a symbol in Judaism and in the Greek culture (Plutarch) and it signified unity and being part of each other.

Even if we find an exact parallel of this ritual outside the Bible in another predating Judaism and Christianity religion (not done yet), still the God whom Christians worship and become part of is absolutely unique—holy, mighty, man (at some point in history), and always God even in man's form, humble, suffering, but always in control, triune. There is no other God like this and taking on His nature, which the Eucharistic meal symbolises is beyond all other achievements and intents of such practices.

Being put to death

Sure, many gods were out to dead but none of them was perfect in holiness, righteousness, purity, power, and love. The fact that Jesus took up human form and died for the sins on the cross makes Him unique. He wasn't killed. He let them kill Him only to resurrect and thus do away with our sins.

The sun becoming dark after the death

This is something all three Synoptic gospels agree on. It may have been mentioned elsewhere, (which is hard to establish) about someone else in the past but again, it is doubtful that it will be close in any significant detail to the event with Jesus.

Darkness for three hours, earthquake and resurrection of people who were dead before is quite a unique phenomenon.
There are many places in the Old Testament where darkening of the Sun is mentioned and it is often ominous. If the New Testament authors experienced or were told about such occurrence, this wouldn't be out of line with the prophetic words revealed so far.

"Who commands the sun not to shine, And sets a seal upon the stars" (Job 6:7).
God can do anything He wishes and in ways more than anyone can imagine.

Rising from the dead

There are examples of rising from the dead in the Old Testament and the people who experienced this all went on to die again. No deity can compare with Jesus' all at once bodily and spiritual resurrection. They all die in dubious circumstances, unlike Jesus, for whom this was prophesied and then come back to live in a strange manner.
Dionysius (the god of wine) was killed and eaten and only his heart was "implanted" in Zeus, so he grew out of his thigh again[46]. This obviously mimics the vine which is cut back in the autumn and grows again in the spring.
Osiris was killed, then put together after being hacked to pieces and then killed again. Finally, he was made the lord of the dead by other deities[47].
Krishna, after living a life of dubious for the Bible morality, was cursed by a man for not ending a bloody war between two clans. Although he initially managed to escape it, but later on the curse seemingly caught up with him and he was killed by a hunter who

---

[46] https://www.britannica.com/topic/Dionysus
[47] https://www.laits.utexas.edu/cairo/teachers/osiris.pdf

thought he is a deer[48]. Then he ascended into heaven[49] but without being resurrected and demonstrated to the living people as with Jesus.

Jesus cannot be cursed, so it cannot affect Him. Jesus was never merely a mortal man who got promoted to be God. He was always God who came to earth and lived a life of showing the greatness, goodness, and holiness of God, which none of those deities can measure up to. His resurrection was real, evidenced and forever. He never dies again as others do. And His death was not an accident in the slightest, but a preordained plan of God who knew that humans' evil would do what is natural to it, but also demonstrated how God's wisdom and power could turn it around for good for all who trust Him.

Talking to the disciples after resurrecting

The way Jesus did it was such that nobody who met Him had any doubts that he was alive. Those people who were so afraid for their lives before were willing to be ostracised, persecuted and even die for the sake of saying to the whole world the reality of His resurrection and how this prophetically fulfils the plan of God for the salvation of all who believe.

Ascension into heaven

Again, the big difference is that He gave proof for His resurrection and then crucially, He sent the Holy Spirit to be with His people forever. Jesus practically came through the Holy Spirit and as long as the church preached His word, the Spirit of God would confirm it by miracles, wonders, baptisms in the Spirit, and salvation of the souls. Jesus also left the church which is the group of believers who thrived against numerous odds and in harsh circumstances because He is with them even to this day.

---

[48] Mani, Vettam (1975). *Puranic Encyclopaedia: A Comprehensive Dictionary With Special Reference to the Epic and Puranic Literature.* Delhi: Motilal Banarsidass. p. 429

[49] *Bhagavata Purana* Book 11, chapter 31

Providing salvation for mankind
There is something unique here about Jesus. He was perfect in everything that He did. His death was special because He as God took up the sins of the world. In a way, God says, "I will take it off you even though it pained me and made me sad because I know that some of you would take this opportunity to be with me forever." His work on earth and on the cross was one beautiful explanation of the love of God toward every individual.

Practically, if we are true to the facts and the details, nobody, ever, can even remotely compare to Jesus - the Son of God and Savior of the world.

(40) TOO MANY PROBLEMS

A true, factual religion represented by a supernatural God would not suffer the number of problems that we see in Christianity. It would be precise, flawless, authentic, transcendent, unmatched, prescient, prophetic, revelatory, internally consistent, and scientifically accurate. In Christianity, we see none of these elements.

The conclusion of an objective analysis is that, beyond a reasonable doubt, Christianity is untrue.

One major lesson to be learned about determining what to believe and what not to believe can be summed up in a few words: The things that are real can be observed, measured, or demonstrated. To that end, we can say confidently that ghosts, goblins, poltergeists, Bigfoot, the Loch Ness Monster, alien abductions, wizards, witches, angels, demons, fairies, and unicorns are not real. And we can add one more item to this list: The God of Christianity

RESPONSE

The faith from God was given to the world in a way of stories and personable discourse. It requires the ardent reading of the Bible and guidance from the Holy Spirit to understand and live out God's truths. Rather than approaching it with arrogance or seeking to poke holes in it, which as we saw leads to misunderstandings and creating a false impression of the Biblical Christianity, one should trust that God wants to reveal

Himself and then look to genuinely figure out what He means in His written Word - the Bible. He didn't give us mathematical formula or a constitution in a legal jargon which would be accessible for only a few. He gave us several different people, stories about them, genres in the collection of 66 books (the Bible) like prose, project, poetry, legal texts, history, epistles and so on, precisely to address the complex human nature and ensure that the core of the Gospel, that Jesus is the Savior from the sins and the oppression of the evil one, is well understood by all people.

The Bible is precise in its own way. It has got a central thrust - it doesn't make sense without Jesus being the centre of the interpretation and the Christian life. The faith which comes through it is flawless because it is neither merely a focus on one's own works and achievements (all other religions emphasise the work of man to get to God), nor is it alleviating the responsibility of men to follow and love God with all their heart and put His words into practice.

In it, we see the glorious love of God toward humanity expressed in and through Jesus Christ of Nazareth. It is authentic and unique because there is no other faith or religion revealing God as so perfect, so great and so humble in His love and commitment to us.

This transcendent and unmatched religion or rather understanding of God, which cannot just come onto the human mind because man-made religions tend to put either too much emphasis on human responsibility and are, therefore, highly legalistic (based on strict, dry, and fallible rules) or on the grace of God, which man is not required to appropriate by obedience (antinomianism[50]).

In other faiths, God is part of the world and the world is god. Or there could be many gods, or God could be impersonal

---

[50] The belief that morality is not important and if you have the right faith all is permissible.

altogether or he may be uninterested with humanity and creation. Or personal but strict and absolute singularity which does not allow for God, who is one and more than one at the same time, in perfect unity. He may be never too close or so close that the human being is god himself. Whilst in Christianity, God is the All in all, separate from creation but the creation dwelling in Him, actively affecting history and the course of the creation; He is the perfect Trinity - One God in three Persons with one will, character, power and love towards each other and the world, one who is close and makes humans be like Him and yet humans are never gods like He is. He is an absolute and one above all, and yet, He is incarnational through the man, Jesus Christ.

This cannot just come to any human mind to device. A religion created by man tends to follow the same patterns of animism, polytheism, pantheism, deism, atheism, or absolute monotheism, but Christianity is indeed original and unique. It is revealing the hopeless state of mankind and the miracle of the blessed hope which comes from God in Christ. Its prophecies come to pass as we speak and the Saviour of the world is fulfilling His purpose for it. It takes into account the multiple facets of human experience and understandings of God, refines them by rejecting or critiquing some and accepting and augmenting others. It clarifies and outlines the purpose of life and is internally consistent and coherent with its preaching about it. This should be appreciated and cherished. God actually speaks to man.

God cannot be observed or measured in a controlled and directed manner as with natural sciences objects because God cannot be controlled or directed by no one, but God is relational and He responds to hearts which are desiring to have a relationship with Him. So God can be experienced and loved with the mind, the heart, the soul and all the power we have. No mythical characters, gods or celebrities for that matter can be compared to His grandeur, uniqueness, and love.

"God is Spirit and those who worship Him should do so in Spirit and truth."
- John 4:24

40 problems with Christianity turn out to be no problem at all.

Notes:

1. I encountered those and read them very much out of curiosity and remained astonished how people who slide back like Mr Runyan did actually very often do not know the Word of God well but arrive at it with their own preconceptions.
http://patheos.com/blogs/friendlyatheist/2014/08/26/40-problems-with-christianity/
2. https://space.com/24054-how-old-is-the-universe.htmlaccessed 22 Oct 2017 accessed 22 Oct 2017
3. https://www.spectator.co.uk/2008/03/if-god-proved-he-existed-i-still-wouldnt-believe-in-him/ accessed on 22 Oct 2017
4. http://www.history.com/this-day-in-history/adolf-hitler-commits-suicide-in-his-underground-bunker accessed on 22 Oct 2017
5. Erhman, Bart. D. A Brief Introduction to the NT, OUP, 2009, p15
6. http://www.jewishvirtuallibrary.org/the-messiah accessed on 22 Oct 2017
7. https://bc.edu/schools/stm/crossroads/resources/birthofjesus/intro/the_dating_of_thegospels.html accessed on 22 Oct 2017
8. Those of us who espouse the traditional view know who most likely they are: Levy or Matthew the tax collector (apostle), Mark (son or close coworker of Apostle Peter), Luke (close co-worker of Apostle Paul and John (apostle).
9. ibid.
10. https://voice.dts.edu/article/wallace-new-testament-manscript-first-century/
11. https://ehrmanblog.org/did-jesus-exist-my-debate-with-robert-price/ accessed 23 Oct 2017
12. http://academia.edu/7738059/Author_of_the_Book_of_Matthew_Argument_and_Debate
13. MItchel, William Ramsay, Lucan and Pauline Studies (1908)
14. http://rowanwilliams.archbishopofcanterbury.org/articles.php/1204/an-introduction-to-st-johns-gospel-st-pauls-theological-centre
15. Ibid

16. http://spu.edu/depts/uc/response/new/2013-spring/bible-theology/jesus-according-to-luke.asp
17. https://www.csun.edu/~hcfll004/romancensus.html
18. Wallace, Sherman Le Roy, Taxation in Egypt from Augustus to Diocletian, PUP
19. Flavius Josephus, Antiquities 20.5.2 10
20. Cf. Berger, Adolf. Encyclopedic Dictionary of Roman Law. The American Philosophical Society. 1953. p 529.
21. Gaius 1.1; quoted in Laurens Winkel, "The Peace Treaties of Westphalia as an Instance of the Reception of Roman Law", in Peace Treaties and International Law in European History, p. 225.
22. Porter, J. R. (2010). The Lost Bible. New York: Metro Books. p. 166.
23. Chapman, John.http://www.newadvent.org/cathen/07268b.htm"Hermas." The Catholic EncyclopediaVol. 7. New York: Robert Appleton Company, 1910. 27 September 2017
24. Chapman, John.http://www.newadvent.org/cathen/07268b.htm"Hermas." The Catholic EncyclopediaVol. 7. New York: Robert Appleton Company, 1910. 27 September 2017
25. A.H.M. Jones, The Herods of Judaea (1938)
26. Flavius Josephus, Jewish War 2.57-59 and Jewish Antiquities 17.273-277
27. "The First Jesus?". National Geographic. Retrieved 5 August 2010.
28. Flavius Josephus, Jewish Antiquities 17.278-284
29. Flavius Josephus, Antiquities 20.5.2 102
30. The gospels, we can see, were very honestly written because if they were tampered or designed to comply with Paul's or anyone's ideas they would spare some details as Matthew 27:46 mentioned above, but they did not; why would you write deliberately to push your views through and not skip stuff which may be "embarrassing"?
31. http://w.astro.berkeley.edu/~dperley/univage/univage.html
32. http://worldometers.info/world-population/world-population-by-year/
33. http://www.worldometers.info/world-population/world-population-by-year/
34. https://www.health.harvard.edu/mind-and-mood/attending-religious-services-linked-to-longer-lives-study-shows

35. This is example of following without controlling or deliberately creating environment which is an object to research which seems to fit with the warning of Deuteronomy 6:16
36. http://www.dailymail.co.uk/news/article-1340497/I-walked-walked-I-felt-like-I-entered-realm-Woman-paralysed-23-years-ago-cured-British-spiritual-healer.html
37. Fr. Paolo O. Pirlo, SHMI (1997). "St. Callistus I". My First Book of Saints. Sons of Holy Mary Immaculate - Quality Catholic Publications. p. 240
38. http://www.hawking.org.uk/the-origin-of-the-universe.html
39. http://www.bbc.co.uk/earth/story/20141106-why-does-anything-exist-at-all
40. http://www.astrosociety.org/publication/a-universe-from-nothing/
41. http://nationalgeographic.com/magazine/2005/05/einstein-relativity-cosmology-space-time-big-bang/
42. http://www.space.com/9593-einstein-biggest-blunder-turns.html
43. Lewis, 1927, p. 99
44. http://anglicansonline.org/basics/nicene.html
45. https://web.stanford.edu/~meehan/donnellyr/summary.html
46. The belief that everything that exists is matter or a function of it
47. https://www.britannica.com/topic/Dionysus
48. https://www.laits.utexas.edu/cairo/teachers/osiris.pdf
49. Mani, Vettam (1975). Puranic Encyclopaedia: A Comprehensive Dictionary With Special Reference to the Epic and Puranic Literature. Delhi: Motilal Banarsidass. p. 429
50. Bhagavata Purana Book 11, chapter 31
51. The belief that morality is not important and if you have the right faith all is permissible.

Printed in Great Britain
by Amazon